NIGHT PRAYERBOOK
Compline
LITURGY OF THE HOURS

NIGHT PRAYERBOOK

Compline

LITURGY OF THE HOURS

SACROS
TOOLS FOR WORSHIP

SHOHOLA, PA
IN ASSOCIATION WITH THE ST. THOMAS MORE
HOUSE OF PRAYER, CRANBERRY, PA

SACROS
TOOLS FOR WORSHIP

Copyright © 2005 SACROS, Inc.
Shohola, Pennsylvania
www.sacros.com

Published with the approval of the Committee on the Liturgy,
United States Conference of Catholic Bishops

ISBN: 978-0-9741748-3-9

Printed in the U.S.A.

CONTENTS

FOREWORD

By Wayne Hepler

Night Prayer—Liturgy of the Hours: "The perfect way to end your day"

Beginning with the publication of the "Constitution on the Sacred Liturgy," the first published document of the Second Vatican Council in the year 1964, the Church began a conscious effort to restore the Liturgy of the Hours (also known as the Divine Office) to its proper place in the Sacred Liturgy as the "the prayer of the whole people of God" (CCC 1175). After the council, the prayer book was revised over a period of seven years and was promulgated by Pope Paul VI in 1970 with a recommendation that it be prayed by all Christ's faithful members, including the laity.

With the publication of his Apostolic Letter *Novo Millenio Ineunte* at the end of the Great Jubilee Year 2000, Pope John Paul II made this effort to promote the Liturgy of the Hours particularly his own. In this letter he announced that he intended to use his forthcoming Wednesday audiences to catechize on the Psalms, which are the heart of the Liturgy of the Hours. He began this catechesis on March 28, 2001, with these words:

> In the Apostolic Letter *"Novo Millenio Ineunte"* I expressed hope that the Church would become more and more distinguished in the "art of prayer" learning it ever anew from the lips of the divine Master. This effort must be expressed above all in the liturgy, the source and summit of ecclesial life. **Consequently, it is important to devote greater pastoral care to promoting the Liturgy of the Hours as a prayer of the whole people of God . . . If, in fact, priests have a precise mandate to celebrate it, it is also warmly recommended to lay people** (emphasis added).

In addition to this catechesis on the Psalms, which he continued for the next four years, Pope John Paul II in his pastoral communications repeatedly reminded the faithful of his desire to see the Liturgy of the Hours restored to its place in the Church's celebration of the Sacred Liturgy. In *"Spirtus et Sponsa"* (the "Spirit and the Bride"), which commemorated the fortieth anniversary of the publication of the "Constitution on the Sacred Liturgy," he challenged the Church to "dare . . . to introduce the faithful to the celebration of the Liturgy of the Hours."

In section eight of *Mane Nobiscum Domine* ("Remain with the Lord"), he repeats his recommendation that the Liturgy of the Hours be used as a tool for "training in prayer."

On January 14, 2005, the Vatican published a Decree from the Apostolic Penitentiary which announced that in conjunction with the Eucharistic Year (October 2004- October 2005) "the Holy Father wished to enrich with indulgences several determined acts of worship and devotion to the Most Holy Sacrament." Included is a Plenary Indulgence for the recitation of Evening Prayer and Night Prayer from the Liturgy of the Hours before the Blessed Sacrament that reads as follows:

> "A Plenary Indulgence is also granted, under the aforesaid conditions, to the clergy, to members of Institutes of Consecrated Life and Societies of Apostolic Life, and to other faithful who are by law obliged to recite the Liturgy of the Hours, as well as to those who customarily recite the Divine Office out of pure devotion, each and every time they recite—at the end of the day, in company or in private—Vespers and Night Prayers before the Lord present in the tabernacle."

It should be obvious by now that Pope John Paul II really wanted all of us to add some part of the Liturgy of the Hours to our discipline of prayer. A reading of Chapter IV of the Constitution on the Sacred Liturgy makes the reasons abundantly clear. **Simply stated, prayed in its approved form, there is no other prayer like the Liturgy of the Hours!** As an inseparable part of the Sacred Liturgy, it is the official public prayer of the Church, offered throughout every day of the liturgical year, making present the very life of Jesus Christ in the celebration of its Seasons, Feasts and Saints, especially in the morning and evening:

> The divine office is devised so that the whole course of the day and night is made holy by the praises of God . . . It is the very prayer which Christ himself, together with his body, addresses to the Father . . . all who render this service . . . are sharing in the greatest honor of Christ's spouse. They are standing before God's throne in the name of the Church their mother . . . interceding for the salvation of the whole world (SC 83-101).

With its balance of adoration, praise, thanksgiving, contemplation, listening and intercessions, the "Hours" are an ideal "school of prayer," uniting personal prayer with the liturgy, by which "the faithful give themselves over to the ministry of love toward God and men, identifying themselves with the action of Christ, who by his life and self-offering sanctified the life of all mankind" (Paul VI).

For those not familiar with praying the "Hours," Night Prayer is a good place to start, and this volume is designed to make it easier. Night Prayer is prayed in a weekly cycle, and except for intercessions, which are unique to Morning and Evening Prayer, has all the elements of the other canonical hours: the Psalms with their antiphons, a short reading from Holy Scripture, a responsory and a Gospel canticle. Because of this, Night Prayer is ideal training in the rubrics and rhythms of liturgical prayer. The tutorial beginning on the next page is offered as a general guide on how to pray the Hours. However, it is not an absolute rule, since various communities recite the Hours a little differently. Because of this, there is no need to worry about doing everything "exactly right."

Night Prayer takes only a few minutes and is an ideal place to start the habit of prayer with one's spouse or family. It is also a beautiful way to extend the short thanksgiving after Holy Communion at an evening Mass, since the Liturgy of the Hours has precisely this finality: it "is like an extension of the Eucharistic celebration" (CCC 1178).

With the opportunity for a short examination of conscience and penitential rite after the introduction, and ending with an antiphon in honor of the blessed Mother, Night Prayer is the perfect way to end your day! Add the Gospel Canticle of Simeon, and when you finish you are not only ready for a good night's sleep, but also for a happy death, as is so aptly summarized by the conclusion:

May the all powerful Lord grant us a restful night and a peaceful death.

— Amen!

How to Use This Book

For those who are new to praying the Liturgy of the Hours, we have included the following tutorial for Night Prayer. As you learn about the various parts of this prayer, you will also be learning how to pray the other Hours of prayer as found in the book *Christian Prayer*. Be aware that the rubrics will vary from place to place. This tutorial is meant to be a guide, but not an absolute rule.

1 **Begin with the Introductory Rite.** Make the sign of the cross when you see the red cross ✠. When there are two or more people praying together, one person recites the line following the red ℣. (= verse). All others present respond with the line following the red ℟. (= response).

Rubrics in brackets are optional, but are normally done when praying with a group.

The alleluia in the Introductory Rite is omitted during Lent.

2 **The Penitential Rite** may be recited after a brief examination of conscience. However, both the examination and the Penitential Rite are optional.

3 **Begin praying the hymn.** The green dot (•) marks off alternating strophes for when two or more people are praying together. The first person or group should pray the first strophe, and the second should follow, continuing to alternate throughout the hymn, changing at every green dot (•).

4 **Begin each psalm or canticle with an antiphon** (noted by the abbreviation Ant., written in green.) One person recites the first word or two of the antiphon and then all join in to recite the rest.

If following the rubrics, all should sit at the beginning of the first psalm until the Reading.

As with the Hymn, when praying the psalm or canticle, the green dot (•) marks off alternating strophes. The first person or group should pray the first strophe, and the second should follow, continuing to alternate, changing at every green dot (•).

Introductory Rite

[STAND] ℣ God, ✠ come to my assistance.
℟ Lord, make haste to help me.
[Bow] • Glory to the Father, and to the Son,
and to the Holy Spirit:
• as it was in the beginning, is now,
and will be for ever. Amen (alleluia).

[A BRIEF EXAMINATION OF CONSCIENCE MAY BE MADE]

Penitential Rite

I confess to almighty God,
and to you, my brothers and sisters,
that I have sinned through my own fault.

[STRIKE BREAST]

in my thoughts and in my words,
in what I have done,
and in what I have failed to do;
and I ask blessed Mary, ever virgin,
all the angels and saints,
and you, my brothers and sisters,
to pray for me to the Lord our God.

℣ May almighty God have mercy on us,
forgive us our sins,
and bring us to everlasting life.

℟ Amen.

Hymn (No. 33)

• O Christ, you are the light and day
Which drives away the night,
The ever shining Sun of God
And pledge of future light.

• As now the ev'ning shadows fall
Please grant us, Lord, we pray,
A quiet night to rest in you
Until the break of day.

• Remember us, poor mortal men,
We humbly ask, O Lord,
And may your presence in our souls,
Be now our great reward.

Translator: Rev. M. Quinn, O.P. et al. 1963

Psalmody

Ant. 1   Have mercy, Lord, and hear my prayer.

Book I: Psalm 4
Thanksgiving
[SIT] • When I call, answer me, O God of justice;

2

SUNDAY VIGIL
Night Prayer

from anguish you released me;
have mercy and hear me!

• O men, how long will your hearts be closed,
will you love what is futile and seek
what is false?

• It is the Lord who grants favors to
those whom he loves;
the Lord hears me whenever I call him.

• Fear him; do not sin: ponder on your bed
and be still.
Make justice your sacrifice and trust
in the Lord.

• "What can bring us happiness?" many say.
Let the light of your face shine on us, O Lord.

• You have put into my heart a greater joy
than they have from abundance of corn
and new wine.

• I will lie down in peace and sleep comes at once
for you alone, Lord, make me dwell in safety.

[Bow] • Glory to the Father, and to the Son,
and to the Holy Spirit:
• as it was in the beginning, is now,
and will be for ever. Amen.

Ant.   Have mercy, Lord, and hear my prayer.

Ant. 2   In the silent hours of night, bless the Lord.

Book 5: Psalm 134
Evening prayer in the Temple
• O come, bless the Lord,
all you who serve the Lord,
who stand in the house of the Lord,
in the courts of the house of our God.

• Lift up your hands to the holy place
and bless the Lord through the night.

• May the Lord bless you from Zion,
he who made both heaven and earth.

[Bow] • Glory to the Father, and to the Son,
and to the Holy Spirit:

---

5 **End each psalm or canticle** by reciting the "Glory to the Father". All should bow their heads (or stand and bow) while the Blessed Trinity is named.

6 After the "Glory to the Father", everyone repeats the antiphon together. If there is a second antiphon and psalm, repeat steps 4 and following.

7 Whoever is leading the prayer stands for the Reading.

8 Recite the Response To The Word of God. If there are two or more present, the versicles (indicated by the symbol ℣.) are recited by the person doing the Reading. All others recite the responses (indicated by the symbol ℟.).

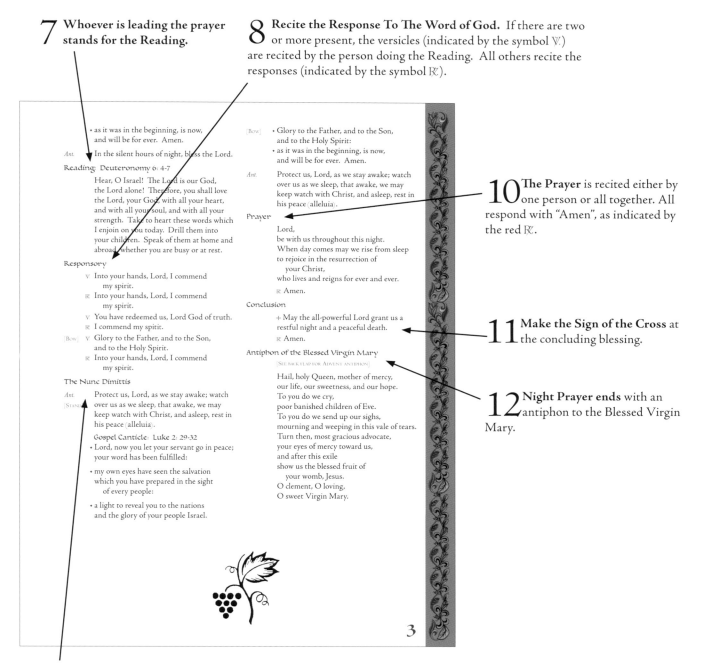

• as it was in the beginning, is now, and will be for ever. Amen.

Ant. In the silent hours of night, bless the Lord.

Reading: Deuteronomy 6: 4-7

Hear, O Israel! The Lord is our God, the Lord alone! Therefore, you shall love the Lord, your God, with all your heart, and with all your soul, and with all your strength. Take to heart these words which I enjoin on you today. Drill them into your children. Speak of them at home and abroad, whether you are busy or at rest.

Responsory

℣ Into your hands, Lord, I commend my spirit.
℟ Into your hands, Lord, I commend my spirit.
℣ You have redeemed us, Lord God of truth.
℟ I commend my spirit.
[Bow] ℣ Glory to the Father, and to the Son, and to the Holy Spirit.
℟ Into your hands, Lord, I commend my spirit.

The Nunc Dimittis

Ant. Protect us, Lord, as we stay awake; watch
[Stand] over us as we sleep, that awake, we may keep watch with Christ, and asleep, rest in his peace (alleluia).

Gospel Canticle: Luke 2: 29-32
• Lord, now you let your servant go in peace; your word has been fulfilled:

• my own eyes have seen the salvation which you have prepared in the sight of every people:

• a light to reveal you to the nations and the glory of your people Israel.

[Bow] • Glory to the Father, and to the Son, and to the Holy Spirit:
• as it was in the beginning, is now, and will be for ever. Amen.

Ant. Protect us, Lord, as we stay awake; watch over us as we sleep, that awake, we may keep watch with Christ, and asleep, rest in his peace (alleluia).

Prayer

Lord,
be with us throughout this night.
When day comes may we rise from sleep to rejoice in the resurrection of your Christ,
who lives and reigns for ever and ever.
℟ Amen.

Conclusion

+ May the all-powerful Lord grant us a restful night and a peaceful death.
℟ Amen.

Antiphon of the Blessed Virgin Mary
[See back flap for Advent antiphon]

Hail, holy Queen, mother of mercy,
our life, our sweetness, and our hope.
To you do we cry,
poor banished children of Eve.
To you do we send up our sighs,
mourning and weeping in this vale of tears.
Turn then, most gracious advocate,
your eyes of mercy toward us,
and after this exile
show us the blessed fruit of
your womb, Jesus.
O clement, O loving,
O sweet Virgin Mary.

3

10 The Prayer is recited either by one person or all together. All respond with "Amen", as indicated by the red ℟.

11 Make the Sign of the Cross at the concluding blessing.

12 Night Prayer ends with an antiphon to the Blessed Virgin Mary.

9 The Gospel Canticle (Nunc Dimittis) follows the same procedure as the psalms and other canticles. It begins with an antiphon, then the canticle is recited either alternating between strophes or in unison, and ends with the antiphon repeated.

Night Prayerbook

Compline

Liturgy of the Hours

Introductory Rite

[Stand] V. God, ✠ come to my assistance.

R. Lord, make haste to help me.

[Bow] ✦ Glory to the Father, and to the Son,
and to the Holy Spirit:

✦ as it was in the beginning, is now,
and will be for ever. Amen (alleluia).

[A brief examination of conscience may be made]

Penitential Rite

I confess to almighty God,
and to you, my brothers and sisters,
that I have sinned through my own fault.

[strike breast]

in my thoughts and in my words,
in what I have done,
and in what I have failed to do;
and I ask blessed Mary, ever virgin,
all the angels and saints,
and you, my brothers and sisters,
to pray for me to the Lord our God.

V. May almighty God have mercy on us,
forgive us our sins,
and bring us to everlasting life.

R. Amen.

Hymn (No. 33)

✦ O Christ, you are the light and day
Which drives away the night,
The ever shining Sun of God
And pledge of future light.

✦ As now the ev'ning shadows fall
Please grant us, Lord, we pray,
A quiet night to rest in you
Until the break of day.

✦ Remember us, poor mortal men,
We humbly ask, O Lord,
And may your presence in our souls,
Be now our great reward.

Translator: Rev. M. Quinn, O.P. et al., 1965

Psalmody

Ant. 1   Have mercy, Lord, and hear my prayer.

Book 1: Psalm 4
Thanksgiving

[Sit] ✦ When I call, answer me, O God of justice;

from anguish you released me;
have mercy and hear me!

✦ O men, how long will your hearts be closed,
will you love what is futile and seek
what is false?

✦ It is the Lord who grants favors to
those whom he loves;
the Lord hears me whenever I call him.

✦ Fear him; do not sin: ponder on your bed
and be still.
Make justice your sacrifice and trust
in the Lord.

✦ "What can bring us happiness?" many say.
Let the light of your face shine on us, O Lord.

✦ You have put into my heart a greater joy
than they have from abundance of corn
and new wine.

✦ I will lie down in peace and sleep comes at once
for you alone, Lord, make me dwell in safety.

[Bow] ✦ Glory to the Father, and to the Son,
and to the Holy Spirit:

✦ as it was in the beginning, is now,
and will be for ever. Amen.

Ant.   Have mercy, Lord, and hear my prayer.

Ant. 2   In the silent hours of night, bless the Lord.

Book 5: Psalm 134
Evening prayer in the Temple

✦ O come, bless the Lord,
all you who serve the Lord,
who stand in the house of the Lord,
in the courts of the house of our God.

✦ Lift up your hands to the holy place
and bless the Lord through the night.

✦ May the Lord bless you from Zion,
he who made both heaven and earth.

[Bow] ✦ Glory to the Father, and to the Son,
and to the Holy Spirit:

+as it was in the beginning, is now,
and will be for ever. Amen.

Ant.   In the silent hours of night, bless the Lord.

Reading: Deuteronomy 6: 4-7

Hear, O Israel! The Lord is our God,
the Lord alone! Therefore, you shall love
the Lord, your God, with all your heart,
and with all your soul, and with all your
strength. Take to heart these words which
I enjoin on you today. Drill them into
your children. Speak of them at home and
abroad, whether you are busy or at rest.

Responsory

℣. Into your hands, Lord, I commend
    my spirit.

℟. Into your hands, Lord, I commend
    my spirit.

℣. You have redeemed us, Lord God of truth.

℟. I commend my spitit.

[Bow] ℣. Glory to the Father, and to the Son,
    and to the Holy Spirit.

℟. Into your hands, Lord, I commend
    my spirit.

The Nunc Dimittis

Ant.   Protect us, Lord, as we stay awake; watch
[Stand] over us as we sleep, that awake, we may
keep watch with Christ, and asleep, rest in
his peace (alleluia).

Gospel Canticle: Luke 2: 29-32

+Lord, now you let your servant go in peace;
your word has been fulfilled:

+my own eyes have seen the salvation
which you have prepared in the sight
of every people:

+a light to reveal you to the nations
and the glory of your people Israel.

[Bow] +Glory to the Father, and to the Son,
and to the Holy Spirit:

+as it was in the beginning, is now,
and will be for ever. Amen.

Ant.   Protect us, Lord, as we stay awake; watch
over us as we sleep, that awake, we may
keep watch with Christ, and asleep, rest in
his peace (alleluia).

Prayer

Lord,
be with us throughout this night.
When day comes may we rise from sleep
to rejoice in the resurrection of
    your Christ,
who lives and reigns for ever and ever.

℟. Amen.

Conclusion

+ May the all-powerful Lord grant us a
restful night and a peaceful death.

℟. Amen.

Antiphon of the Blessed Virgin Mary

[See back flap for Advent antiphon]

Hail, holy Queen, mother of mercy,
our life, our sweetness, and our hope.
To you do we cry,
poor banished children of Eve.
To you do we send up our sighs,
mourning and weeping in this vale of tears.
Turn then, most gracious advocate,
your eyes of mercy toward us,
and after this exile
show us the blessed fruit of
    your womb, Jesus.
O clement, O loving,
O sweet Virgin Mary.

Introductory Rite

[STAND] ℣. God, ✠ come to my assistance.

℟. Lord, make haste to help me.

[BOW] ✦ Glory to the Father, and to the Son,
and to the Holy Spirit:

✦ as it was in the beginning, is now,
and will be for ever. Amen (alleluia).

[A BRIEF EXAMINATION OF CONSCIENCE MAY BE MADE]

Penitential Rite

I confess to almighty God,
and to you, my brothers and sisters,
that I have sinned through my own fault.

[STRIKE BREAST]

in my thoughts and in my words,
in what I have done,
and in what I have failed to do;
and I ask blessed Mary, ever virgin,
all the angels and saints,
and you, my brothers and sisters,
to pray for me to the Lord our God.

℣. May almighty God have mercy on us,
forgive us our sins,
and bring us to everlasting life.

℟. Amen.

Hymn (No. 34)

✦ Lord Jesus Christ, abide with us,
Now that the sun has run its course;
Let hope not be obscured by night,
But may faith's darkness be as light.

✦ Lord Jesus Christ, grant us your peace,
And when the trials of earth shall cease;
Grant us the morning light of grace,
The radiant splendor of your face.

✦ Immortal, Holy Threefold Light,
Yours be the kingdom, pow'r, and might;
All glory be eternally
To you, life giving Trinity.

Text: *Mane Nobiscum Domine*, paraphrased by Jerome
Leaman, 1967

Psalmody

Ant. Night holds no terrors for me sleeping
under God's wings.

SUNDAY
Night Prayer

Book 4: Psalm 91
Safe in God's sheltering care

[SIT] ✦ He who dwells in the shelter of the most High
and abides in the shade of the Almighty
says to the Lord "My refuge,
my stronghold, my God in whom in I trust!"

✦ It is he who will free you from the snare
of the fowler who seeks to destroy you;
he will conceal you with his pinions
and under his wings you will find refuge.

✦ You will not fear the terror of the night
nor the arrow that flies by day,
nor the plague that prowls in the darkness
nor the scourge that lays waste at noon.

✦ A thousand may fall at your side,
ten thousand fall at your right,
you, it will never approach;
his faithfulness is buckler and shield.

✦ Your eyes have only to look
to see how the wicked are repaid,
you who have said: "Lord, my refuge!"
and have made the Most High your dwelling.

✦ Upon you no evil shall fall,
no plague approach where you dwell.
For you has he commanded his angels,
to keep you in all your ways.

✦ They shall bear you upon their hands
lest you strike your foot against a stone.
On the lion and the viper you will tread
and trample the young lion and the dragon.

✦ Since he clings to me in love, I will free him;
protect him for he knows my name.
When he calls I shall answer: "I am with you."
I will save him in distress and give him glory.

✦ With length of life I will content him;
I shall let him see my saving power.

[Bow] + Glory to the Father, and to the Son,
and to the Holy Spirit:

+ as it was in the beginning, is now,
and will be for ever. Amen.

Ant. Night holds no terrors for me sleeping
under God's wings.

Reading: Revelation 22: 4-5

They shall see him face to face and bear
his name on their foreheads. The night
shall be no more. They will need no light
from lamps or the sun, for the Lord God
shall give them light, and they shall reign
forever.

Responsory

℣. Into your hands, Lord, I commend
my spirit.

℟. Into your hands, Lord, I commend
my spirit.

℣. You have redeemed us, Lord God of truth.

℟. I commend my spirit.

[Bow] ℣. Glory to the Father, and to the Son,
and to the Holy Spirit.

℟. Into your hands, Lord, I commend
my spirit.

The Nunc Dimittis

Ant.
[Stand] Protect us, Lord, as we stay awake; watch
over us as we sleep, that awake, we may
keep watch with Christ, and asleep, rest in
his peace (alleluia).

Gospel Canticle: Luke 2: 29-32

+ Lord, now you let your servant go in peace;
your word has been fulfilled:

+ my own eyes have seen the salvation
which you have prepared in the sight
of every people:

+ a light to reveal you to the nations
and the glory of your people Israel.

[Bow] + Glory to the Father, and to the Son,
and to the Holy Spirit:

+ as it was in the beginning, is now,
and will be for ever. Amen.

Ant. Protect us, Lord, as we stay awake; watch
over us as we sleep, that awake, we may
keep watch with Christ, and asleep, rest in
his peace (alleluia).

Prayer

Lord,
we have celebrated today
the mystery of the rising of Christ
to new life.
May we now rest in your peace,
safe from all that could harm us,
and rise again refreshed and joyful,
to praise you throughout another day.
We ask this through Christ our Lord.

℟. Amen.

Conclusion

+ May the all-powerful Lord grant us a
restful night and a peaceful death.

℟. Amen.

Antiphon of the Blessed Virgin Mary

[See back flap for Advent antiphon]

Hail, holy Queen, mother of mercy,
our life, our sweetness, and our hope.
To you do we cry,
poor banished children of Eve.
To you do we send up our sighs,
mourning and weeping in this vale of tears.
Turn then, most gracious advocate,
your eyes of mercy toward us,
and after this exile
show us the blessed fruit of
your womb, Jesus.
O clement, O loving,
O sweet Virgin Mary.

Introductory Rite

[STAND] V. God, ✠ come to my assistance.

R. Lord, make haste to help me.

[BOW] ✦ Glory to the Father, and to the Son,
and to the Holy Spirit:

✦ as it was in the beginning, is now,
and will be for ever. Amen (alleluia).

[A BRIEF EXAMINATION OF CONSCIENCE MAY BE MADE]

Penitential Rite

I confess to almighty God,
and to you, my brothers and sisters,
that I have sinned through my own fault.

[STRIKE BREAST]

in my thoughts and in my words,
in what I have done,
and in what I have failed to do;
and I ask blessed Mary, ever virgin,
all the angels and saints,
and you, my brothers and sisters,
to pray for me to the Lord our God.

V. May almighty God have mercy on us,
forgive us our sins,
and bring us to everlasting life.

R. Amen.

Hymn (No. 33)

✦ O Christ, you are the light and day
Which drives away the night,
The ever shining Sun of God
And pledge of future light.

✦ As now the ev'ning shadows fall
Please grant us, Lord, we pray,
A quiet night to rest in you
Until the break of day.

✦ Remember us, poor mortal men,
We humbly ask, O Lord,
And may your presence in our souls,
Be now our great reward.

Translator: Rev. M. Quinn, O.P. et al., 1965

Psalmody

Ant. O Lord, our God, unwearied is your love
for us.

Book 3: Psalm 86
'Poor man's prayer in trouble'

[SIT] ✦ Turn your ear, O Lord, and give answer

for I am poor and needy.
Preserve my life, for I am faithful:
save the servant who trusts in you.

✦ You are my God; have mercy on me, Lord,
for I cry to you all day long.
Give joy to your servant, O Lord,
for to you I lift up my soul.

✦ O Lord, you are good and forgiving,
full of love to all who call.
Give heed, O Lord, to my prayer
and attend to the sound of my voice.

✦ In the day of distress I will call
and surely you will reply.
Among the gods there is none like you, O Lord;
nor work to compare with yours.

✦ All the nations shall come to adore you
and glorify your name, O Lord:
for you are great and do marvellous deeds,
you who alone are God.

✦ Show me, Lord, your way
so that I may walk in your truth.
Guide my heart to fear your name.

✦ I will praise you, Lord my God, with all my heart
and glorify your name for ever;
for your love to me has been great:
you have saved me from the depths of the grave.

✦ The proud have risen against me;
ruthless men seek my life:
to you they pay no heed.

✦ But you, God of mercy and compassion,
slow to anger, O Lord,
abounding in love and truth,
turn and take pity on me.

✦ O give your strength to your servant
and save your handmaid's son.
Show me a sign of your favor
that my foes may see to their shame
that you console me and give me your help.

[Bow] + Glory to the Father, and to the Son,
and to the Holy Spirit:

+ as it was in the beginning, is now,
and will be for ever. Amen.

Ant. O Lord, our God, unwearied is your love
for us.

Reading: 1 Thessalonians 5: 9-10

God has destined us for acquiring
salvation through our Lord Jesus Christ.
He died for us, that all of us, whether
awake or asleep, together might live with
him.

Responsory

℣. Into your hands, Lord, I commend
my spirit.

℞. Into your hands, Lord, I commend
my spirit.

℣. You have redeemed us, Lord God of truth.

℞. I commend my spitit.

[Bow] ℣. Glory to the Father, and to the Son,
and to the Holy Spirit.

℞. Into your hands, Lord, I commend
my spirit.

The Nunc Dimittis

Ant. Protect us, Lord, as we stay awake; watch
[Stand] over us as we sleep, that awake, we may
keep watch with Christ, and asleep, rest in
his peace (alleluia).

Gospel Canticle: Luke 2: 29-32

+ Lord, now you let your servant go in peace;
your word has been fulfilled:

+ my own eyes have seen the salvation
which you have prepared in the sight
of every people:

+ a light to reveal you to the nations

and the glory of your people Israel.

[Bow] + Glory to the Father, and to the Son,
and to the Holy Spirit:

+ as it was in the beginning, is now,
and will be for ever. Amen.

Ant. Protect us, Lord, as we stay awake; watch
over us as we sleep, that awake, we may
keep watch with Christ, and asleep, rest in
his peace (alleluia).

Prayer

Lord,
give our bodies restful sleep
and let the work we have done today
bear fruit in eternal life.
We ask this through Christ our Lord.

℞. Amen.

Conclusion

+ May the all-powerful Lord grant us a
restful night and a peaceful death.

℞. Amen.

Antiphon of the Blessed Virgin Mary

[See back flap for Advent antiphon]

Hail, holy Queen, mother of mercy,
our life, our sweetness, and our hope.
To you do we cry,
poor banished children of Eve.
To you do we send up our sighs,
mourning and weeping in this vale of tears.
Turn then, most gracious advocate,
your eyes of mercy toward us,
and after this exile
show us the blessed fruit of
your womb, Jesus.
O clement, O loving,
O sweet Virgin Mary.

7

Introductory Rite

[STAND] V. God, ✠ come to my assistance.

R. Lord, make haste to help me.

[BOW] ✦ Glory to the Father, and to the Son,
and to the Holy Spirit:

✦ as it was in the beginning, is now,
and will be for ever. Amen (alleluia).

[A BRIEF EXAMINATION OF CONSCIENCE MAY BE MADE]

Penitential Rite

I confess to almighty God,
and to you, my brothers and sisters,
that I have sinned through my own fault.

[STRIKE BREAST]

in my thoughts and in my words,
in what I have done,
and in what I have failed to do;
and I ask blessed Mary, ever virgin,
all the angels and saints,
and you, my brothers and sisters,
to pray for me to the Lord our God.

V. May almighty God have mercy on us,
forgive us our sins,
and bring us to everlasting life.

R. Amen.

Hymn (No. 34)

✦ Lord Jesus Christ, abide with us,
Now that the sun has run its course;
Let hope not be obscured by night,
But may faith's darkness be as light.

✦ Lord Jesus Christ, grant us your peace,
And when the trials of earth shall cease;
Grant us the morning light of grace,
The radiant splendor of your face.

✦ Immortal, Holy Threefold Light,
Yours be the kingdom, pow'r, and might;
All glory be eternally
To you, life giving Trinity.

Text: *Mane Nobiscum Domine*, paraphrased by Jerome
Leaman, 1967

Psalmody

Ant. Do not hide your face from me; in you I
put my trust.

TUESDAY
Night Prayer

Book 5: Psalm 143: 1-11
Prayer in distress

[SIT] ✦ Lord, listen to my prayer:
turn your ear to my appeal.
You are faithful, you are just; give answer.
Do not call your servant to judgment
for no one is just in your sight.

✦ The enemy pursues my soul;
he has crushed my life to the ground;
he has made me dwell in darkness
like the dead, long forgotten.
Therefore my spirit fails;
my heart is numb within me.

✦ I remember the days that are past:
I ponder all your works.
I muse on what your hand has wrought
and to you I stretch out my hands.
Like a parched land my soul thirsts for you.

✦ Lord, make haste and answer;
for my spirit fails within me.
Do not hide your face
lest I become like those in the grave.

✦ In the morning let me know your love
for I put my trust in you.
Make me know the way I should walk:
to you I lift up my soul.

✦ Rescue me, Lord, from my enemies;
I have fled to you for refuge.
Teach me to do your will
for you, O Lord, are my God.
Let your good spirit guide me
in ways that are level and smooth.

✦ For your name's sake, Lord, save my life;
in your justice save my soul from distress.

[BOW] ✦ Glory to the Father, and to the Son,
and to the Holy Spirit:

+ as it was in the beginning, is now,
and will be for ever. Amen.

Ant. Do not hide your face from me; in you I
put my trust.

Reading: 1 Peter 5: 8-9a

Stay sober and alert. Your opponent the
devil is prowling like a roaring lion looking
for someone to devour. Resist him, solid
in your faith.

Responsory

℣. Into your hands, Lord, I commend
my spirit.

℟. Into your hands, Lord, I commend
my spirit.

℣. You have redeemed us, Lord God of truth.

℟. I commend my spitit.

[Bow] ℣. Glory to the Father, and to the Son,
and to the Holy Spirit.

℟. Into your hands, Lord, I commend
my spirit.

The Nunc Dimittis

Ant. Protect us, Lord, as we stay awake; watch
[Stand] over us as we sleep, that awake, we may
keep watch with Christ, and asleep, rest in
his peace (alleluia).

Gospel Canticle: Luke 2: 29-32

+ Lord, now you let your servant go in peace;
your word has been fulfilled:

+ my own eyes have seen the salvation
which you have prepared in the sight
of every people:

+ a light to reveal you to the nations
and the glory of your people Israel.

[Bow] + Glory to the Father, and to the Son,
and to the Holy Spirit:

+ as it was in the beginning, is now,
and will be for ever. Amen.

Ant. Protect us, Lord, as we stay awake; watch
over us as we sleep, that awake, we may
keep watch with Christ, and asleep, rest in
his peace (alleluia).

Prayer

Lord,
fill this night with your radiance.
May we sleep in peace and rise with joy
to welcome the light of a new day
in your name.
We ask this through Christ our Lord.

℟. Amen.

Conclusion

+ May the all-powerful Lord grant us a
restful night and a peaceful death.

℟. Amen.

Antiphon of the Blessed Virgin Mary

[See back flap for Advent antiphon]

Hail, holy Queen, mother of mercy,
our life, our sweetness, and our hope.
To you do we cry,
poor banished children of Eve.
To you do we send up our sighs,
mourning and weeping in this vale of tears.
Turn then, most gracious advocate,
your eyes of mercy toward us,
and after this exile
show us the blessed fruit of
your womb, Jesus.
O clement, O loving,
O sweet Virgin Mary.

Introductory Rite

[STAND] V. God, ✠ come to my assistance.
R. Lord, make haste to help me.

[BOW] ✦ Glory to the Father, and to the Son,
and to the Holy Spirit:
✦ as it was in the beginning, is now,
and will be for ever. Amen (alleluia).

[A BRIEF EXAMINATION OF CONSCIENCE MAY BE MADE]

Penitential Rite

I confess to almighty God,
and to you, my brothers and sisters,
that I have sinned through my own fault.

[STRIKE BREAST]

in my thoughts and in my words,
in what I have done,
and in what I have failed to do;
and I ask blessed Mary, ever virgin,
all the angels and saints,
and you, my brothers and sisters,
to pray for me to the Lord our God.

V. May almighty God have mercy on us,
forgive us our sins,
and bring us to everlasting life.

R. Amen.

Hymn (No. 33)

✦ O Christ, you are the light and day
Which drives away the night,
The ever shining Sun of God
And pledge of future light.

✦ As now the ev'ning shadows fall
Please grant us, Lord, we pray,
A quiet night to rest in you
Until the break of day.

✦ Remember us, poor mortal men,
We humbly ask, O Lord,
And may your presence in our souls,
Be now our great reward.

Translator: Rev. M. Quinn, O.P. et al., 1965

Psalmody

Ant. 1 Lord God, be my refuge and my strength.

Book 1: Psalm 31: 1-6
Trustful prayer in adversity

[SIT] ✦ In you, O Lord, I take refuge.

WEDNESDAY
Night Prayer

Let me never be put to shame.
In your justice, set me free,
hear me and speedily rescue me.

✦ Be a rock of refuge for me,
a mighty stronghold to save me,
for you are my rock, my stronghold.
For your name's sake, lead me and guide me.

✦ Release me from the snares they have hidden
for you are my refuge, Lord.
Into your hands I commend my spirit.
It is you who will redeem me, Lord.

[BOW] ✦ Glory to the Father, and to the Son,
and to the Holy Spirit:
✦ as it was in the beginning, is now,
and will be for ever. Amen.

Ant. Lord God, be my refuge and my strength.

Ant. 2 Out of the depths I cry to you, Lord.

Book 5: Psalm 130
A cry from the depths

[SIT] ✦ Out of the depths I cry to you, O Lord,
Lord, hear my voice!
O let your ears be attentive
to the voice of my pleading.

✦ If you, O Lord, should mark our guilt,
Lord, who would survive?
But with you is found forgiveness:
for this we revere you.

✦ My soul is waiting for the Lord.
I count on his word.
My soul is longing for the Lord
more than watchman for daybreak.
Let the watchman count on daybreak
and Israel on the Lord.

✦ Because with the Lord there is mercy
and fullness of redemption,
Israel indeed he will redeem
from all its iniquity.

10

[Bow] ✦ Glory to the Father, and to the Son,
and to the Holy Spirit:
✦ as it was in the beginning, is now,
and will be for ever. Amen.

Ant.   Out of the depths I cry to you, Lord.

Reading: Ephesians 4: 26-27

If you are angry, let it be without sin. The sun must not go down on your wrath; do not give the devil a chance to work on you.

Responsory

℣. Into your hands, Lord, I commend my spirit.

℟. Into your hands, Lord, I commend my spirit.

℣. You have redeemed us, Lord God of truth.

℟. I commend my spitit.

[Bow] ℣. Glory to the Father, and to the Son, and to the Holy Spirit.

℟. Into your hands, Lord, I commend my spirit.

The Nunc Dimittis

Ant.
[Stand]   Protect us, Lord, as we stay awake; watch over us as we sleep, that awake, we may keep watch with Christ, and asleep, rest in his peace (alleluia).

Gospel Canticle: Luke 2: 29-32

✦ Lord, now you let your servant go in peace; your word has been fulfilled:

✦ my own eyes have seen the salvation which you have prepared in the sight of every people:

✦ a light to reveal you to the nations and the glory of your people Israel.

[Bow] ✦ Glory to the Father, and to the Son, and to the Holy Spirit:

as it was in the beginning, is now, and will be for ever. Amen.

Ant.   Protect us, Lord, as we stay awake; watch over us as we sleep, that awake, we may keep watch with Christ, and asleep, rest in his peace (alleluia).

Prayer

Lord Jesus Christ,
you have given your followers
an example of gentleness and humility,
a task that is easy, a burden that is light.
Accept the prayers and work of this day,
and give us the rest that will strengthen us
to render more faithful service to you
who live and reign for ever and ever.

℟ Amen.

Conclusion

✠ May the all-powerful Lord grant us a restful night and a peaceful death.

℟ Amen.

Antiphon of the Blessed Virgin Mary

[See back flap for Advent antiphon]

Hail, holy Queen, mother of mercy,
our life, our sweetness, and our hope.
To you do we cry,
poor banished children of Eve.
To you do we send up our sighs,
mourning and weeping in this vale of tears.
Turn then, most gracious advocate,
your eyes of mercy toward us,
and after this exile
show us the blessed fruit of your womb,
Jesus.
O clement, O loving,
O sweet Virgin Mary.

11

Introductory Rite

[Stand] V. God, ✠ come to my assistance.

℟. Lord, make haste to help me.

[Bow] ✦ Glory to the Father, and to the Son,
and to the Holy Spirit:

✦ as it was in the beginning, is now,
and will be for ever. Amen (alleluia).

[A brief examination of conscience may be made]

Penitential Rite

I confess to almighty God,
and to you, my brothers and sisters,
that I have sinned through my own fault.

[Strike breast]

in my thoughts and in my words,
in what I have done,
and in what I have failed to do;
and I ask blessed Mary, ever virgin,
all the angels and saints,
and you, my brothers and sisters,
to pray for me to the Lord our God.

V. May almighty God have mercy on us,
forgive us our sins,
and bring us to everlasting life.

℟. Amen.

Hymn (No. 34)

✦ Lord Jesus Christ, abide with us,
Now that the sun has run its course;
Let hope not be obscured by night,
But may faith's darkness be as light.

✦ Lord Jesus Christ, grant us your peace,
And when the trials of earth shall cease;
Grant us the morning light of grace,
The radiant splendor of your face.

✦ Immortal, Holy Threefold Light,
Yours be the kingdom, pow'r, and might;
All glory be eternally
To you, life giving Trinity.

Text: *Mane Nobiscum Domine*, paraphrased by Jerome
Leaman, 1967

Psalmody

Ant. In you, my God, my body will rest in hope.

Book 1: Psalm 16
God is my portion, my inheritance

[Sit] ✦ Preserve me, God, I take refuge in you.

THURSDAY
Night Prayer

I say to the Lord: "You are my God.
My happiness lies in you alone."

✦ He has put into my heart a marvelous love
for the faithful ones who dwell in his land.
Those who choose other gods increase
their sorrows.
Never will I offer their offerings of blood.
Never will I take their name upon my lips.

✦ O Lord, it is you who are my
portion and cup;
it is you yourself who are my prize.
The lot marked out for me is my delight:
welcome indeed the heritage that falls to me!

✦ I will bless the Lord who gives me counsel,
who even at night directs my heart.
I keep the Lord ever in my sight:
since he is at my right hand,
I shall stand firm.

✦ And so my heart rejoices, my soul is glad;
even my body shall rest in safety.
For you will not leave my soul
among the dead,
nor let your beloved know decay.

✦ You will show me the path of life,
the fullness of joy in your presence,
at your right hand happiness for ever.

[Bow] ✦ Glory to the Father, and to the Son,
and to the Holy Spirit:

✦ as it was in the beginning, is now,
and will be for ever. Amen.

Ant. In you, my God, my body will rest in hope.

Reading: 1 Thessalonians 5: 23

May the God of peace make you perfect in
holiness. May he preserve you whole and
entire, spirit, soul, and body, irreproachable
at the coming of our Lord Jesus Christ.

Responsory

V. Into your hands, Lord, I commend my spirit.

R. Into your hands, Lord, I commend my spirit.

V. You have redeemed us, Lord God of truth.

R. I commend my spirit.

[Bow] V. Glory to the Father, and to the Son, and to the Holy Spirit.

R. Into your hands, Lord, I commend my spirit.

The Nunc Dimittis

Ant.

[Stand] Protect us, Lord, as we stay awake; watch over us as we sleep, that awake, we may keep watch with Christ, and asleep, rest in his peace (alleluia).

Gospel Canticle: Luke 2: 29-32

✦ Lord, now you let your servant go in peace; your word has been fulfilled:

✦ my own eyes have seen the salvation which you have prepared in the sight of every people:

✦ a light to reveal you to the nations and the glory of your people Israel.

[Bow] ✦ Glory to the Father, and to the Son, and to the Holy Spirit:

✦ as it was in the beginning, is now, and will be for ever. Amen.

Ant. Protect us, Lord, as we stay awake; watch over us as we sleep, that awake, we may keep watch with Christ, and asleep, rest in his peace (alleluia).

Prayer

Lord God,
send peaceful sleep
to refresh our tired bodies.
May your help always renew us
and keep us strong in your service.
We ask this through Christ our Lord.

R. Amen.

Conclusion

✛ May the all-powerful Lord grant us a restful night and a peaceful death.

R. Amen.

Antiphon of the Blessed Virgin Mary

[See back flap for Advent antiphon]

Hail, holy Queen, mother of mercy,
our life, our sweetness, and our hope.
To you do we cry,
poor banished children of Eve.
To you do we send up our sighs,
mourning and weeping in this vale of tears.
Turn then, most gracious advocate,
your eyes of mercy toward us,
and after this exile
show us the blessed fruit of
    your womb, Jesus.
O clement, O loving,
O sweet Virgin Mary.

Introductory Rite

[Stand] V. God, ✠ come to my assistance.

R. Lord, make haste to help me.

[Bow] ✦ Glory to the Father, and to the Son,
and to the Holy Spirit:

✦ as it was in the beginning, is now,
and will be for ever. Amen (alleluia).

[A brief examination of conscience may be made]

Penitential Rite

I confess to almighty God,
and to you, my brothers and sisters,
that I have sinned through my own fault.

[Strike breast]

in my thoughts and in my words,
in what I have done,
and in what I have failed to do;
and I ask blessed Mary, ever virgin,
all the angels and saints,
and you, my brothers and sisters,
to pray for me to the Lord our God.

V. May almighty God have mercy on us,
forgive us our sins,
and bring us to everlasting life.

R. Amen.

Hymn (No. 33)

✦ O Christ, you are the light and day
Which drives away the night,
The ever shining Sun of God
And pledge of future light.

✦ As now the ev'ning shadows fall
Please grant us, Lord, we pray,
A quiet night to rest in you
Until the break of day.

✦ Remember us, poor mortal men,
We humbly ask, O Lord,
And may your presence in our souls,
Be now our great reward.

Translator: Rev. M. Quinn, O.P. et al., 1965

Psalmody

Ant. Day and night I cry to you, my God.

Book 3: Psalm 88
Prayer of a sick person

[Sit] ✦ Lord my God, I call for help by day;

FRIDAY
Night Prayer

I cry at night before you.
Let my prayer come into your presence.
O turn your ear to my cry.

✦ For my soul is filled with evils;
my life is on the brink of the grave.
I am reckoned as one in the tomb:
I have reached the end of my strength,

✦ like one alone among the dead;
like the slain lying in their graves;
like those you remember no more,
cut off, as they are, from your hand.

✦ You have laid me in the depths of the tomb,
in places that are dark, in the depths.
Your anger weighs down upon me:
I am drowned beneath your waves.

✦ You have taken away my friends
and made me hateful in their sight.
Imprisoned, I cannot escape;
my eyes are sunken with grief.

✦ I call to you, Lord, all the day long;
to you I stretch out my hands.
Will you work your wonders for the dead?
Will the shades stand and praise you?

✦ Will your love be told in the grave
or your faithfulness among the dead?
Will your wonders be known in the dark
or your justice in the land of oblivion?

✦ As for me, Lord, I call to you for help:
in the morning my prayer comes before you.
Lord, why do you reject me?
Why do you hide your face?

✦ Wretched, close to death from my youth,
I have borne your trials; I am numb.
Your fury has swept down upon me;
your terrors have utterly destroyed me.

✦ They surround me all the day like a flood,
they assail me all together.

Friend and neighbor you have taken away:
my one companion is darkness.

[Bow] ✦ Glory to the Father, and to the Son,
and to the Holy Spirit:
✦ as it was in the beginning, is now,
and will be for ever. Amen.

Ant. Day and night I cry to you, my God.

Reading: Jeremiah 14: 9a

You are in our midst, O Lord,
your name we bear;
do not forsake us, O Lord, our God!

Responsory

℣. Into your hands, Lord, I commend
my spirit.
℟. Into your hands, Lord, I commend
my spirit.
℣. You have redeemed us, Lord God of truth.
℟. I commend my spitit.
[Bow] ℣. Glory to the Father, and to the Son,
and to the Holy Spirit.
℟. Into your hands, Lord, I commend
my spirit.

The Nunc Dimittis

Ant.
[Stand] Protect us, Lord, as we stay awake; watch
over us as we sleep, that awake, we may
keep watch with Christ, and asleep, rest in
his peace (alleluia).

Gospel Canticle: Luke 2: 29-32

✦ Lord, now you let your servant go in peace;
your word has been fulfilled:

✦ my own eyes have seen the salvation
which you have prepared in the sight
of every people:

✦ a light to reveal you to the nations

and the glory of your people Israel.

[Bow] ✦ Glory to the Father, and to the Son,
and to the Holy Spirit:
✦ as it was in the beginning, is now,
and will be for ever. Amen.

Ant. Protect us, Lord, as we stay awake; watch
over us as we sleep, that awake, we may
keep watch with Christ, and asleep, rest in
his peace (alleluia).

Prayer

All-powerful God,
keep us united with your Son
in his death and burial
so that we may rise to new life with him,
who lives and reigns for ever and ever.

℟. Amen.

Conclusion

✛ May the all-powerful Lord grant us a
restful night and a peaceful death.
℟. Amen.

Antiphon of the Blessed Virgin Mary

[See back flap for Advent antiphon]

Hail, holy Queen, mother of mercy,
our life, our sweetness, and our hope.
To you do we cry,
poor banished children of Eve.
To you do we send up our sighs,
mourning and weeping in this vale of tears.
Turn then, most gracious advocate,
your eyes of mercy toward us,
and after this exile
show us the blessed fruit of
your womb, Jesus.
O clement, O loving,
O sweet Virgin Mary.

15

THE SACRED TRIDUUM

HOLY THURSDAY, GOOD FRIDAY, HOLY SATURDAY

Introductory Rite

[STAND] V. God, ✠ come to my assistance.

R. Lord, make haste to help me.

[BOW] ✦ Glory to the Father, and to the Son,
and to the Holy Spirit:

✦ as it was in the beginning, is now,
and will be for ever. Amen.

[A BRIEF EXAMINATION OF CONSCIENCE MAY BE MADE]

Penitential Rite

I confess to almighty God,
and to you, my brothers and sisters,
that I have sinned through my own fault.

[STRIKE BREAST]

in my thoughts and in my words,
in what I have done,
and in what I have failed to do;
and I ask blessed Mary, ever virgin,
all the angels and saints,
and you, my brothers and sisters,
to pray for me to the Lord our God.

V. May almighty God have mercy on us,
forgive us our sins,
and bring us to everlasting life.

R. Amen.

Hymn (No. 34)

✦ Lord Jesus Christ, abide with us,
Now that the sun has run its course;
Let hope not be obscured by night,
But may faith's darkness be as light.

✦ Lord Jesus Christ, grant us your peace,
And when the trials of earth shall cease;
Grant us the morning light of grace,
The radiant splendor of your face.

✦ Immortal, Holy Threefold Light,
Yours be the kingdom, pow'r, and might;
All glory be eternally
To you, life giving Trinity.

Text: *Mane Nobiscum Domine*, paraphrased by Jerome
Leaman, 1967

Psalmody

Ant. Night holds no terrors for me sleeping under
God's wings.

HOLY THURSDAY
Night Prayer

Book 4: Psalm 91
Safe in God's sheltering care

[SIT] ✦ He who dwells in the shelter of the most High
and abides in the shade of the Almighty
says to the Lord "My refuge,
my stronghold, my God in whom in I trust!"

✦ It is he who will free you from the snare
of the fowler who seeks to destroy you;
he will conceal you with his pinions
and under his wings you will find refuge.

✦ You will not fear the terror of the night
nor the arrow that flies by day,
nor the plague that prowls in the darkness
nor the scourge that lays waste at noon.

✦ A thousand may fall at your side,
ten thousand fall at your right,
you, it will never approach;
his faithfulness is buckler and shield.

✦ Your eyes have only to look
to see how the wicked are repaid,
you who have said: "Lord, my refuge!"
and have made the Most High your dwelling.

✦ Upon you no evil shall fall,
no plague approach where you dwell.
For you has he commanded his angels,
to keep you in all your ways.

✦ They shall bear you upon their hands
lest you strike your foot against a stone.
On the lion and the viper you will tread
and trample the young lion and the dragon.

✦ Since he clings to me in love, I will free him;
protect him for he knows my name.
When he calls I shall answer: "I am with you."
I will save him in distress and give him glory.

✦ With length of life I will content him;
I shall let him see my saving power.

[Bow] ✛ Glory to the Father, and to the Son,
and to the Holy Spirit:
✛ as it was in the beginning, is now,
and will be for ever. Amen.

Ant.   Night holds no terrors for me sleeping
under God's wings.

Reading: Revelation 22: 4-5

They shall see him face to face and bear
his name on their foreheads. The night
shall be no more. They will need no light
from lamps or the sun, for the Lord God
shall give them light, and they shall reign
forever.

Ant.   For our sake Christ was obedient,
accepting even death.

The Nunc Dimittis

Ant.   Protect us, Lord, as we stay awake; watch
[Stand]   over us as we sleep, that awake, we may
keep watch with Christ, and asleep, rest in
his peace.

Gospel Canticle: Luke 2: 29-32

✛ Lord, now you let your servant go in peace;
your word has been fulfilled:

✛ my own eyes have seen the salvation
which you have prepared in the sight
of every people:

✛ a light to reveal you to the nations
and the glory of your people Israel.

[Bow] ✛ Glory to the Father, and to the Son,
and to the Holy Spirit:
✛ as it was in the beginning, is now,
and will be for ever. Amen.

Ant.   Protect us, Lord, as we stay awake; watch
over us as we sleep, that awake, we may keep
watch with Christ, and asleep, rest in his
peace.

Prayer

Lord,
we beg you to visit this house
and banish from it
all the deadly power of the enemy.
May your holy angels dwell here
to keep us in peace,
and may your blessing be upon us always.
We ask this through Christ our Lord.

℟ Amen.

Conclusion

✛ May the all-powerful Lord grant us a
restful night and a peaceful death.

℟ Amen.

Antiphon of the Blessed Virgin Mary

Hail, holy Queen, mother of mercy,
our life, our sweetness, and our hope.
To you do we cry,
poor banished children of Eve.
To you do we send up our sighs,
mourning and weeping in this vale of tears.
Turn then, most gracious advocate,
your eyes of mercy toward us,
and after this exile
show us the blessed fruit of
your womb, Jesus.
O clement, O loving,
O sweet Virgin Mary.

19

Introductory Rite

[Stand] V. God, ✠ come to my assistance.

R. Lord, make haste to help me.

[Bow] ✦ Glory to the Father, and to the Son,
and to the Holy Spirit:

✦ as it was in the beginning, is now,
and will be for ever. Amen.

[A brief examination of conscience may be made]

Penitential Rite

I confess to almighty God,
and to you, my brothers and sisters,
that I have sinned through my own fault.

[Strike breast]

in my thoughts and in my words,
in what I have done,
and in what I have failed to do;
and I ask blessed Mary, ever virgin,
all the angels and saints,
and you, my brothers and sisters,
to pray for me to the Lord our God.

V. May almighty God have mercy on us,
forgive us our sins,
and bring us to everlasting life.

R. Amen.

Hymn (No. 34)

✦ Lord Jesus Christ, abide with us,
Now that the sun has run its course;
Let hope not be obscured by night,
But may faith's darkness be as light.

✦ Lord Jesus Christ, grant us your peace,
And when the trials of earth shall cease;
Grant us the morning light of grace,
The radiant splendor of your face.

✦ Immortal, Holy Threefold Light,
Yours be the kingdom, pow'r, and might;
All glory be eternally
To you, life giving Trinity.

Text: *Mane Nobiscum Domine*, paraphrased by Jerome
Leaman, 1967

Psalmody

Ant. Night holds no terrors for me sleeping
under God's wings.

GOOD FRIDAY
Night Prayer

Book 4: Psalm 91
Safe in God's sheltering care

[Sit] ✦ He who dwells in the shelter of the most High
and abides in the shade of the Almighty
says to the Lord "My refuge,
my stronghold, my God in whom in I trust!"

✦ It is he who will free you from the snare
of the fowler who seeks to destroy you;
he will conceal you with his pinions
and under his wings you will find refuge.

✦ You will not fear the terror of the night
nor the arrow that flies by day,
nor the plague that prowls in the darkness
nor the scourge that lays waste at noon.

✦ A thousand may fall at your side,
ten thousand fall at your right,
you, it will never approach;
his faithfulness is buckler and shield.

✦ Your eyes have only to look
to see how the wicked are repaid,
you who have said: "Lord, my refuge!"
and have made the Most High your dwelling.

✦ Upon you no evil shall fall,
no plague approach where you dwell.
For you has he commanded his angels,
to keep you in all your ways.

✦ They shall bear you upon their hands
lest you strike your foot against a stone.
On the lion and the viper you will tread
and trample the young lion and the dragon.

✦ Since he clings to me in love, I will free him;
protect him for he knows my name.
When he calls I shall answer: "I am with you."
I will save him in distress and give him glory.

✦ With length of life I will content him;
I shall let him see my saving power.

[Bow] + Glory to the Father, and to the Son,
and to the Holy Spirit:
+ as it was in the beginning, is now,
and will be for ever. Amen.

Ant. Night holds no terrors for me sleeping
under God's wings.

Reading: Revelation 22: 4-5

They shall see him face to face and bear
his name on their foreheads. The night
shall be no more. They will need no light
from lamps or the sun, for the Lord God
shall give them light, and they shall reign
forever.

Ant. For our sake Christ was obedient,
accepting even death, death on a cross.

The Nunc Dimittis

Ant. Protect us, Lord, as we stay awake; watch
[Stand] over us as we sleep, that awake, we may
keep watch with Christ, and asleep, rest in
his peace.

Gospel Canticle: Luke 2: 29-32

+ Lord, now you let your servant go in peace;
your word has been fulfilled:

+ my own eyes have seen the salvation
which you have prepared in the sight
of every people:

+ a light to reveal you to the nations
and the glory of your people Israel.

[Bow] + Glory to the Father, and to the Son,
and to the Holy Spirit:
+ as it was in the beginning, is now,
and will be for ever. Amen.

Ant. Protect us, Lord, as we stay awake; watch
over us as we sleep, that awake, we may keep
watch with Christ, and asleep, rest in his
peace.

Prayer

Lord,
we beg you to visit this house
and banish from it
all the deadly power of the enemy.
May your holy angels dwell here
to keep us in peace,
and may your blessing be upon us always.
We ask this through Christ our Lord.

℟ Amen.

Conclusion

+ May the all-powerful Lord grant us a
restful night and a peaceful death.

℟ Amen.

Antiphon of the Blessed Virgin Mary

Hail, holy Queen, mother of mercy,
our life, our sweetness, and our hope.
To you do we cry,
poor banished children of Eve.
To you do we send up our sighs,
mourning and weeping in this vale of tears.
Turn then, most gracious advocate,
your eyes of mercy toward us,
and after this exile
show us the blessed fruit of
your womb, Jesus.
O clement, O loving,
O sweet Virgin Mary.

21

Introductory Rite

[STAND] V. God, ✠ come to my assistance.

R. Lord, make haste to help me.

[BOW] ✤ Glory to the Father, and to the Son,
and to the Holy Spirit:

✤ as it was in the beginning, is now,
and will be for ever. Amen.

[A BRIEF EXAMINATION OF CONSCIENCE MAY BE MADE]

Penitential Rite

I confess to almighty God,
and to you, my brothers and sisters,
that I have sinned through my own fault.

[STRIKE BREAST]

in my thoughts and in my words,
in what I have done,
and in what I have failed to do;
and I ask blessed Mary, ever virgin,
all the angels and saints,
and you, my brothers and sisters,
to pray for me to the Lord our God.

V. May almighty God have mercy on us,
forgive us our sins,
and bring us to everlasting life.

R. Amen.

Hymn (No. 34)

✤ Lord Jesus Christ, abide with us,
Now that the sun has run its course;
Let hope not be obscured by night,
But may faith's darkness be as light.

✤ Lord Jesus Christ, grant us your peace,
And when the trials of earth shall cease;
Grant us the morning light of grace,
The radiant splendor of your face.

✤ Immortal, Holy Threefold Light,
Yours be the kingdom, pow'r, and might;
All glory be eternally
To you, life giving Trinity.

Text: *Mane Nobiscum Domine*, paraphrased by Jerome
Leaman, 1967

Psalmody

Ant. Night holds no terrors for me sleeping
under God's wings.

HOLY SATURDAY
Night Prayer

FOR THOSE WHO ATTEND, THE
EASTER VIGIL REPLACES HOLY
SATURDAY NIGHT PRAYER.

Book 4: Psalm 91

Safe in God's sheltering care

[SIT] ✤ He who dwells in the shelter of the most High
and abides in the shade of the Almighty
says to the Lord "My refuge,
my stronghold, my God in whom in I trust!"

✤ It is he who will free you from the snare
of the fowler who seeks to destroy you;
he will conceal you with his pinions
and under his wings you will find refuge.

✤ You will not fear the terror of the night
nor the arrow that flies by day,
nor the plague that prowls in the darkness
nor the scourge that lays waste at noon.

✤ A thousand may fall at your side,
ten thousand fall at your right,
you, it will never approach;
his faithfulness is buckler and shield.

✤ Your eyes have only to look
to see how the wicked are repaid,
you who have said: "Lord, my refuge!"
and have made the Most High your dwelling.

✤ Upon you no evil shall fall,
no plague approach where you dwell.
For you has he commanded his angels,
to keep you in all your ways.

✤ They shall bear you upon their hands
lest you strike your foot against a stone.
On the lion and the viper you will tread
and trample the young lion and the dragon.

✤ Since he clings to me in love, I will free him;
protect him for he knows my name.
When he calls I shall answer: "I am with you."
I will save him in distress and give him glory.

✤ With length of life I will content him;
I shall let him see my saving power.

[Bow]   + Glory to the Father, and to the Son,
and to the Holy Spirit:
+ as it was in the beginning, is now,
and will be for ever. Amen.

Ant.   Night holds no terrors for me sleeping
under God's wings.

Reading: Revelation 22: 4-5

They shall see him face to face and bear
his name on their foreheads. The night
shall be no more. They will need no light
from lamps or the sun, for the Lord God
shall give them light, and they shall reign
forever.

Ant.   For our sake Christ was obedient,
accepting even death, death on a cross.
Therefore God raised him on high and
gave him the name above all other names.

The Nunc Dimittis

Ant.   Protect us, Lord, as we stay awake; watch
[STAND]   over us as we sleep, that awake, we may
keep watch with Christ, and asleep, rest in
his peace.

Gospel Canticle: Luke 2: 29-32

+ Lord, now you let your servant go in peace;
your word has been fulfilled:

+ my own eyes have seen the salvation
which you have prepared in the sight
of every people:

+ a light to reveal you to the nations
and the glory of your people Israel.

[Bow]   + Glory to the Father, and to the Son,
and to the Holy Spirit:
+ as it was in the beginning, is now,
and will be for ever. Amen.

Ant.   Protect us, Lord, as we stay awake; watch
over us as we sleep, that awake, we may keep
watch with Christ, and asleep, rest in his
peace.

Prayer

Lord,
we beg you to visit this house
and banish from it
all the deadly power of the enemy.
May your holy angels dwell here
to keep us in peace,
and may your blessing be upon us always.
We ask this through Christ our Lord.

℟ Amen.

Conclusion

+ May the all-powerful Lord grant us a
restful night and a peaceful death.

℟ Amen.

Antiphon of the Blessed Virgin Mary

Hail, holy Queen, mother of mercy,
our life, our sweetness, and our hope.
To you do we cry,
poor banished children of Eve.
To you do we send up our sighs,
mourning and weeping in this vale of tears.
Turn then, most gracious advocate,
your eyes of mercy toward us,
and after this exile
show us the blessed fruit of
your womb, Jesus.
O clement, O loving,
O sweet Virgin Mary.

23

EASTER OCTAVE

EASTER SUNDAY THROUGH
THE SECOND SUNDAY OF EASTER

DURING THE EASTER OCTAVE,

USE "OPTION I" OR "OPTION II"

FROM THE FOLLOWING PAGES.

THESE MAY BE PRAYED ALTERNATELY THROUGHOUT THE OCTAVE.

Introductory Rite

[STAND] V. God, ✠ come to my assistance.

℟. Lord, make haste to help me.

[BOW] ✦ Glory to the Father, and to the Son,
and to the Holy Spirit:

✦ as it was in the beginning, is now,
and will be for ever. Amen, alleluia.

[A BRIEF EXAMINATION OF CONSCIENCE MAY BE MADE]

Penitential Rite

I confess to almighty God,
and to you, my brothers and sisters,
that I have sinned through my own fault.

[STRIKE BREAST]

in my thoughts and in my words,
in what I have done,
and in what I have failed to do;
and I ask blessed Mary, ever virgin,
all the angels and saints,
and you, my brothers and sisters,
to pray for me to the Lord our God.

V. May almighty God have mercy on us,
forgive us our sins,
and bring us to everlasting life.

℟. Amen.

Hymn (No. 34)

✦ Lord Jesus Christ, abide with us,
Now that the sun has run its course;
Let hope not be obscured by night,
But may faith's darkness be as light.

✦ Lord Jesus Christ, grant us your peace,
And when the trials of earth shall cease;
Grant us the morning light of grace,
The radiant splendor of your face.

✦ Immortal, Holy Threefold Light,
Yours be the kingdom, pow'r, and might;
All glory be eternally
To you, life giving Trinity.

Text: *Mane Nobiscum Domine*, paraphrased by Jerome
Leaman, 1967

Psalmody

Ant.   Alleluia, alleluia, alleluia.

EASTER OCTAVE
Night Prayer
OPTION I

Book 4: Psalm 91
Safe in God's sheltering care

[SIT] ✦ He who dwells in the shelter of the most High
and abides in the shade of the Almighty
says to the Lord "My refuge,
my stronghold, my God in whom in I trust!"

✦ It is he who will free you from the snare
of the fowler who seeks to destroy you;
he will conceal you with his pinions
and under his wings you will find refuge.

✦ You will not fear the terror of the night
nor the arrow that flies by day,
nor the plague that prowls in the darkness
nor the scourge that lays waste at noon.

✦ A thousand may fall at your side,
ten thousand fall at your right,
you, it will never approach;
his faithfulness is buckler and shield.

✦ Your eyes have only to look
to see how the wicked are repaid,
you who have said: "Lord, my refuge!"
and have made the Most High your dwelling.

✦ Upon you no evil shall fall,
no plague approach where you dwell.
For you has he commanded his angels,
to keep you in all your ways.

✦ They shall bear you upon their hands
lest you strike your foot against a stone.
On the lion and the viper you will tread
and trample the young lion and the dragon.

✦ Since he clings to me in love, I will free him;
protect him for he knows my name.
When he calls I shall answer: "I am with you."
I will save him in distress and give him glory.

✦ With length of life I will content him;
I shall let him see my saving power.

[Bow] ✠ Glory to the Father, and to the Son,
and to the Holy Spirit:
✠ as it was in the beginning, is now,
and will be for ever. Amen.

Ant. Alleluia, alleluia, alleluia.

Reading: Revelation 22: 4-5

They shall see him face to face and bear his name on their foreheads. The night shall be no more. They will need no light from lamps or the sun, for the Lord God shall give them light, and they shall reign forever.

Ant. This is the day the Lord has made; let us rejoice and be glad, alleluia.

The Nunc Dimittis

Ant.
[Stand] Protect us, Lord, as we stay awake; watch over us as we sleep, that awake, we may keep watch with Christ, and asleep, rest in his peace, alleluia.

Gospel Canticle: Luke 2: 29-32

✠ Lord, now you let your servant go in peace; your word has been fulfilled:

✠ my own eyes have seen the salvation which you have prepared in the sight of every people:

✠ a light to reveal you to the nations and the glory of your people Israel.

[Bow] ✠ Glory to the Father, and to the Son,
and to the Holy Spirit:
✠ as it was in the beginning, is now,
and will be for ever. Amen.

Ant. Protect us, Lord, as we stay awake; watch over us as we sleep, that awake, we may keep watch with Christ, and asleep, rest in his peace, alleluia.

Prayer

Lord,
we have celebrated today
the mystery of the rising of Christ to new life.
May we now rest in your peace,
safe from all that could harm us,
and rise again refreshed and joyful,
to praise you throughout another day.
We ask this through Christ our Lord.

℟ Amen.

Conclusion

✠ May the all-powerful Lord grant us a restful night and a peaceful death.
℟ Amen.

Antiphon of the Blessed Virgin Mary

Queen of heaven, rejoice, alleluia.
The Son whom you merited to bear, alleluia,
has risen as he said, alleluia.
Pray to God for us, alleluia.

Rejoice and be glad, O Virgin Mary, alleluia.
For the Lord has truly risen, alleluia.

Introductory Rite

[STAND] V. God, ✠ come to my assistance.
R. Lord, make haste to help me.

[Bow] ✦ Glory to the Father, and to the Son,
and to the Holy Spirit:
✦ as it was in the beginning, is now,
and will be for ever. Amen, alleluia.

[A BRIEF EXAMINATION OF CONSCIENCE MAY BE MADE]

Penitential Rite

I confess to almighty God,
and to you, my brothers and sisters,
that I have sinned through my own fault.

[STRIKE BREAST]

in my thoughts and in my words,
in what I have done,
and in what I have failed to do;
and I ask blessed Mary, ever virgin,
all the angels and saints,
and you, my brothers and sisters,
to pray for me to the Lord our God.

V. May almighty God have mercy on us,
forgive us our sins,
and bring us to everlasting life.

R. Amen.

Hymn (No. 33)

✦ O Christ, you are the light and day
Which drives away the night,
The ever shining Sun of God
And pledge of future light.

✦ As now the ev'ning shadows fall
Please grant us, Lord, we pray,
A quiet night to rest in you
Until the break of day.

✦ Remember us, poor mortal men,
We humbly ask, O Lord,
And may your presence in our souls,
Be now our great reward.

Translator: Rev. M. Quinn, O.P. et al., 1965

Psalmody

Ant. 1   Alleluia, alleluia, alleluia.

Book 1: Psalm 4
Thanksgiving

[SIT] ✦ When I call, answer me, O God of justice;

EASTER OCTAVE
Night Prayer
OPTION II

from anguish you released me; have mercy and
hear me!

✦ O men, how long will your hearts be closed,
will you love what is futile and seek what is
false?

✦ It is the Lord who grants favors to those whom
he loves;
the Lord hears me whenever I call him.

✦ Fear him; do not sin: ponder on your bed and
be still.
Make justice your sacrifice and trust in the
Lord.

✦ "What can bring us happiness?" many say.
Let the light of your face shine on us, O Lord.

✦ You have put into my heart a greater joy
than they have from abundance of corn and
new wine.

✦ I will lie down in peace and sleep comes at once
for you alone, Lord, make me dwell in safety.

[Bow] ✦ Glory to the Father, and to the Son,
and to the Holy Spirit:
✦ as it was in the beginning, is now,
and will be for ever. Amen.

Book 5: Psalm 134
Evening prayer in the Temple

✦ O come, bless the Lord,
all you who serve the Lord,
who stand in the house of the Lord,
in the courts of the house of our God.

✦ Lift up your hands to the holy place
and bless the Lord through the night.

✦ May the Lord bless you from Zion,
he who made both heaven and earth.

[Bow] ✦ Glory to the Father, and to the Son,
and to the Holy Spirit:
✦ as it was in the beginning, is now,
and will be for ever. Amen.

Ant. Alleluia, alleluia, alleluia.

Reading: Deuteronomy 6: 4-7

Hear, O Israel! The Lord is our God, the Lord alone! Therefore, you shall love the Lord, your God, with all your heart, and with all your soul, and with all your strength. Take to heart these words which I enjoin on you today. Drill them into your children. Speak of them at home and abroad, whether you are busy or at rest.

Ant. This is the day the Lord has made; let us rejoice and be glad, alleluia.

The Nunc Dimittis

Ant.
[STAND]

Protect us, Lord, as we stay awake; watch over us as we sleep, that awake, we may keep watch with Christ, and asleep, rest in his peace, alleluia.

Gospel Canticle: Luke 2: 29-32

+ Lord, now you let your servant go in peace; your word has been fulfilled:

+ my own eyes have seen the salvation which you have prepared in the sight of every people:

+ a light to reveal you to the nations and the glory of your people Israel.

[BOW] + Glory to the Father, and to the Son, and to the Holy Spirit:

+ as it was in the beginning, is now,

and will be for ever. Amen.

Ant. Protect us, Lord, as we stay awake; watch over us as we
sleep, that awake, we may keep watch with Christ, and asleep, rest in his peace, alleluia.

Prayer

Lord,
be with us throughout this night.
When day comes may we rise from sleep to rejoice in the resurrection of your Christ, who lives and reigns for ever and ever.

℟ Amen.

Conclusion

+ May the all-powerful Lord grant us a restful night and a peaceful death.

℟ Amen.

Antiphon of the Blessed Virgin Mary

Queen of heaven, rejoice, alleluia.
The Son whom you merited to bear, alleluia,
has risen as he said, alleluia.
Pray to God for us, alleluia.

Rejoice and be glad, O Virgin Mary, alleluia.
For the Lord has truly risen, alleluia.

Easter Season

Monday after the Easter Octave
Through Pentecost Sunday

Introductory Rite

[STAND] V. God, ✠ come to my assistance.

℟. Lord, make haste to help me.

[BOW] ✦ Glory to the Father, and to the Son,
and to the Holy Spirit:

✦ as it was in the beginning, is now,
and will be for ever. Amen, alleluia.

[A BRIEF EXAMINATION OF CONSCIENCE MAY BE MADE]

Penitential Rite

I confess to almighty God,
and to you, my brothers and sisters,
that I have sinned through my own fault.

[STRIKE BREAST]

in my thoughts and in my words,
in what I have done,
and in what I have failed to do;
and I ask blessed Mary, ever virgin,
all the angels and saints,
and you, my brothers and sisters,
to pray for me to the Lord our God.

V. May almighty God have mercy on us,
forgive us our sins,
and bring us to everlasting life.

℟. Amen.

Hymn (No. 33)

✦ O Christ, you are the light and day
Which drives away the night,
The ever shining Sun of God
And pledge of future light.

✦ As now the ev'ning shadows fall
Please grant us, Lord, we pray,
A quiet night to rest in you
Until the break of day.

✦ Remember us, poor mortal men,
We humbly ask, O Lord,
And may your presence in our souls,
Be now our great reward.

Translator: Rev. M. Quinn, O.P. et al., 1965

Psalmody

Ant. Alleluia, alleluia, alleluia.

Book 3: Psalm 86
'Poor man's prayer in trouble'

[SIT] ✦ Turn your ear, O Lord, and give answer
for I am poor and needy.

MONDAY IN EASTER SEASON
Night Prayer

Preserve my life, for I am faithful:
save the servant who trusts in you.

✦ You are my God; have mercy on me, Lord,
for I cry to you all day long.
Give joy to your servant, O Lord,
for to you I lift up my soul.

✦ O Lord, you are good and forgiving,
full of love to all who call.
Give heed, O Lord, to my prayer
and attend to the sound of my voice.

✦ In the day of distress I will call
and surely you will reply.
Among the gods there is none like you, O Lord;
nor work to compare with yours.

✦ All the nations shall come to adore you
and glorify your name, O Lord:
for you are great and do marvellous deeds,
you who alone are God.

✦ Show me, Lord, your way
so that I may walk in your truth.
Guide my heart to fear your name.

✦ I will praise you, Lord my God, with all my heart
and glorify your name for ever;
for your love to me has been great:
you have saved me from the depths of the grave.

✦ The proud have risen against me;
ruthless men seek my life:
to you they pay no heed.

✦ But you, God of mercy and compassion,
slow to anger, O Lord,
abounding in love and truth,
turn and take pity on me.

✦ O give your strength to your servant
and save your handmaid's son.
Show me a sign of your favor
that my foes may see to their shame
that you console me and give me your help.

[BOW] ✦ Glory to the Father, and to the Son,

and to the Holy Spirit:
+ as it was in the beginning, is now,
and will be for ever. Amen.

Ant.   Alleluia, alleluia, alleluia.

Reading: 1 Thessalonians 5: 9-10

God has destined us for acquiring
salvation through our Lord Jesus Christ.
He died for us, that all of us, whether
awake or asleep, together might live with
him.

Responsory

℣. Into your hands, Lord, I commend
my spirit, alleluia, alleluia.
℟. Into your hands, Lord, I commend
my spirit, alleluia, alleluia.
℣. You have redeemed us, Lord God of truth.
℟. Alleluia, alleluia.
[Bow] ℣. Glory to the Father, and to the Son,
and to the Holy Spirit.
℟. Into your hands, Lord, I commend
my spirit, alleluia, alleluia.

The Nunc Dimittis

Ant.   Protect us, Lord, as we stay awake; watch
[Stand] over us as we sleep, that awake, we may
keep watch with Christ, and asleep, rest in
his peace, alleluia.

Gospel Canticle: Luke 2: 29-32
+ Lord, now you let your servant go in peace;
your word has been fulfilled:

+ my own eyes have seen the salvation

which you have prepared in the sight
of every people:

+ a light to reveal you to the nations
and the glory of your people Israel.

[Bow] + Glory to the Father, and to the Son,
and to the Holy Spirit:
+ as it was in the beginning, is now,
and will be for ever. Amen.

Ant.   Protect us, Lord, as we stay awake; watch
over us as we sleep, that awake, we may keep
watch with Christ, and asleep, rest in his
peace, alleluia.

Prayer

Lord,
give our bodies restful sleep
and let the work we have done today
bear fruit in eternal life.
We ask this through Christ our Lord.

℟. Amen.

Conclusion

+ May the all-powerful Lord grant us a
restful night and a peaceful death.
℟. Amen.

Antiphon of the Blessed Virgin Mary

Queen of heaven, rejoice, alleluia.
The Son whom you merited to bear, alleluia,
has risen as he said, alleluia.
Pray to God for us, alleluia.

Rejoice and be glad, O Virgin Mary, alleluia.
For the Lord has truly risen, alleluia.

Introductory Rite

[STAND] V. God, ✠ come to my assistance.

R. Lord, make haste to help me.

[BOW] ✢ Glory to the Father, and to the Son,
and to the Holy Spirit:

✢ as it was in the beginning, is now,
and will be for ever. Amen, alleluia.

[A BRIEF EXAMINATION OF CONSCIENCE MAY BE MADE]

Penitential Rite

I confess to almighty God,
and to you, my brothers and sisters,
that I have sinned through my own fault.

[STRIKE BREAST]

in my thoughts and in my words,
in what I have done,
and in what I have failed to do;
and I ask blessed Mary, ever virgin,
all the angels and saints,
and you, my brothers and sisters,
to pray for me to the Lord our God.

V. May almighty God have mercy on us,
forgive us our sins,
and bring us to everlasting life.

R. Amen.

Hymn (No. 34)

✢ Lord Jesus Christ, abide with us,
Now that the sun has run its course;
Let hope not be obscured by night,
But may faith's darkness be as light.

✢ Lord Jesus Christ, grant us your peace,
And when the trials of earth shall cease;
Grant us the morning light of grace,
The radiant splendor of your face.

✢ Immortal, Holy Threefold Light,
Yours be the kingdom, pow'r, and might;
All glory be eternally
To you, life giving Trinity.

Text: *Mane Nobiscum Domine*, paraphrased by Jerome
Leaman, 1967

Psalmody

Ant. Alleluia, alleluia, alleluia.

Book 5: Psalm 143: 1-11
Prayer in distress

[SIT] ✢ Lord, listen to my prayer:

TUESDAY IN EASTER SEASON
Night Prayer

turn your ear to my appeal.
You are faithful, you are just; give answer.
Do not call your servant to judgment
for no one is just in your sight.

✦ The enemy pursues my soul;
he has crushed my life to the ground;
he has made me dwell in darkness
like the dead, long forgotten.
Therefore my spirit fails;
my heart is numb within me.

✦ I remember the days that are past:
I ponder all your works.
I muse on what your hand has wrought
and to you I stretch out my hands.
Like a parched land my soul thirsts for you.

✦ Lord, make haste and answer;
for my spirit fails within me.
Do not hide your face
lest I become like those in the grave.

✦ In the morning let me know your love
for I put my trust in you.
Make me know the way I should walk:
to you I lift up my soul.

✦ Rescue me, Lord, from my enemies;
I have fled to you for refuge.
Teach me to do your will
for you, O Lord, are my God.
Let your good spirit guide me
in ways that are level and smooth.

✦ For your name's sake, Lord, save my life;
in your justice save my soul from distress.

[BOW] ✦ Glory to the Father, and to the Son,
and to the Holy Spirit:

✦ as it was in the beginning, is now,
and will be for ever. Amen.

Ant. Alleluia, alleluia, alleluia.

Reading: 1 Peter 5: 8-9a

Stay sober and alert. Your opponent the devil is prowling like a roaring lion looking for someone to devour. Resist him, solid in your faith.

Responsory

V. Into your hands, Lord, I commend my spirit, alleluia, alleluia.

R. Into your hands, Lord, I commend my spirit, alleluia, alleluia.

V. You have redeemed us, Lord God of truth.

R. Alleluia, alleluia.

[Bow] V. Glory to the Father, and to the Son, and to the Holy Spirit.

R. Into your hands, Lord, I commend my spirit, alleluia, alleluia.

The Nunc Dimittis

Ant. Protect us, Lord, as we stay awake; watch
[Stand] over us as we sleep, that awake, we may keep watch with Christ, and asleep, rest in his peace, alleluia.

Gospel Canticle: Luke 2: 29-32

+ Lord, now you let your servant go in peace; your word has been fulfilled:

+ my own eyes have seen the salvation which you have prepared in the sight of every people:

+ a light to reveal you to the nations and the glory of your people Israel.

[Bow] + Glory to the Father, and to the Son, and to the Holy Spirit:

+ as it was in the beginning, is now, and will be for ever. Amen.

Ant. Protect us, Lord, as we stay awake; watch over us as we sleep, that awake, we may keep watch with Christ, and asleep, rest in his peace, alleluia.

Prayer

Lord,
fill this night with your radiance.
May we sleep in peace and rise with joy
to welcome the light of a new day in your name.
We ask this through Christ our Lord.

R. Amen.

Conclusion

+ May the all-powerful Lord grant us a restful night and a peaceful death.

R. Amen.

Antiphon of the Blessed Virgin Mary

Queen of heaven, rejoice, alleluia.
The Son whom you merited to bear, alleluia,
has risen as he said, alleluia.
Pray to God for us, alleluia.

Rejoice and be glad, O Virgin Mary, alleluia.
For the Lord has truly risen, alleluia.

Introductory Rite

[STAND] V. God, ✠ come to my assistance.

R. Lord, make haste to help me.

[BOW] Glory to the Father, and to the Son,
and to the Holy Spirit:

✦ as it was in the beginning, is now,
and will be for ever. Amen, alleluia.

[A BRIEF EXAMINATION OF CONSCIENCE MAY BE MADE]

Penitential Rite

I confess to almighty God,
and to you, my brothers and sisters,
that I have sinned through my own fault.

[STRIKE BREAST]

in my thoughts and in my words,
in what I have done,
and in what I have failed to do;
and I ask blessed Mary, ever virgin,
all the angels and saints,
and you, my brothers and sisters,
to pray for me to the Lord our God.

V. May almighty God have mercy on us,
forgive us our sins,
and bring us to everlasting life.

R. Amen.

Hymn (No. 33)

✦ O Christ, you are the light and day
Which drives away the night,
The ever shining Sun of God
And pledge of future light.

✦ As now the ev'ning shadows fall
Please grant us, Lord, we pray,
A quiet night to rest in you
Until the break of day.

✦ Remember us, poor mortal men,
We humbly ask, O Lord,
And may your presence in our souls,
Be now our great reward.

Translator: Rev. M. Quinn, O.P. et al., 1965

Psalmody

Ant. Alleluia, alleluia, alleluia.

Book 1: Psalm 31: 1-6
Trustful prayer in adversity

[SIT] ✦ In you, O Lord, I take refuge.

WEDNESDAY IN EASTER SEASON
Night Prayer

Let me never be put to shame.
In your justice, set me free,
hear me and speedily rescue me.

✦ Be a rock of refuge for me,
a mighty stronghold to save me,
for you are my rock, my stronghold.
For your name's sake, lead me and guide me.

✦ Release me from the snares they have hidden
for you are my refuge, Lord.
Into your hands I commend my spirit.
It is you who will redeem me, Lord.

[BOW] ✦ Glory to the Father, and to the Son,
and to the Holy Spirit:

✦ as it was in the beginning, is now,
and will be for ever. Amen.

Book 5: Psalm 130
A cry from the depths

[SIT] ✦ Out of the depths I cry to you, O Lord,
Lord, hear my voice!
O let your ears be attentive
to the voice of my pleading.

✦ If you, O Lord, should mark our guilt,
Lord, who would survive?
But with you is found forgiveness:
for this we revere you.

✦ My soul is waiting for the Lord.
I count on his word.
My soul is longing for the Lord
more than watchman for daybreak.
Let the watchman count on daybreak
and Israel on the Lord.

✦ Because with the Lord there is mercy
and fullness of redemption,
Israel indeed he will redeem
from all its iniquity.

[BOW] ✦ Glory to the Father, and to the Son,
and to the Holy Spirit:

+ as it was in the beginning, is now,
and will be for ever. Amen.

Ant. Alleluia, alleluia, alleluia.

Reading: Ephesians 4: 26-27

If you are angry, let it be without sin. The sun must not go down on your wrath; do not give the devil a chance to work on you.

Responsory

℣. Into your hands, Lord, I commend my spirit, alleluia, alleluia.

℟. Into your hands, Lord, I commend my spirit, alleluia, alleluia.

℣. You have redeemed us, Lord God of truth.

℟. Alleluia, alleluia.

[Bow] ℣. Glory to the Father, and to the Son, and to the Holy Spirit.

℟. Into your hands, Lord, I commend my spirit, alleluia, alleluia.

The Nunc Dimittis

Ant.
[Stand] Protect us, Lord, as we stay awake; watch over us as we sleep, that awake, we may keep watch with Christ, and asleep, rest in his peace, alleluia.

Gospel Canticle: Luke 2: 29-32

+ Lord, now you let your servant go in peace; your word has been fulfilled:

+ my own eyes have seen the salvation which you have prepared in the sight of every people:

+ a light to reveal you to the nations and the glory of your people Israel.

[Bow] + Glory to the Father, and to the Son, and to the Holy Spirit:

+ as it was in the beginning, is now, and will be for ever. Amen.

Ant. Protect us, Lord, as we stay awake; watch over us as we sleep, that awake, we may keep watch with Christ, and asleep, rest in his peace, alleluia.

Prayer

Lord Jesus Christ,
you have given your followers
an example of gentleness and humility,
a task that is easy, a burden that is light.
Accept the prayers and work of this day,
and give us the rest that will strengthen us
to render more faithful service to you
who live and reign for ever and ever.

℟ Amen.

Conclusion

+ May the all-powerful Lord grant us a restful night and a peaceful death.

℟ Amen.

Antiphon of the Blessed Virgin Mary

Queen of heaven, rejoice, alleluia.
The Son whom you merited to bear, alleluia,
has risen as he said, alleluia.
Pray to God for us, alleluia.

Rejoice and be glad, O Virgin Mary, alleluia.
For the Lord has truly risen, alleluia.

Introductory Rite

[STAND] V. God, ✠ come to my assistance.

R. Lord, make haste to help me.

[BOW] + Glory to the Father, and to the Son,
and to the Holy Spirit:

+ as it was in the beginning, is now,
and will be for ever. Amen, alleluia.

[A BRIEF EXAMINATION OF CONSCIENCE MAY BE MADE]

Penitential Rite

I confess to almighty God,
and to you, my brothers and sisters,
that I have sinned through my own fault.

[STRIKE BREAST]

in my thoughts and in my words,
in what I have done,
and in what I have failed to do;
and I ask blessed Mary, ever virgin,
all the angels and saints,
and you, my brothers and sisters,
to pray for me to the Lord our God.

V. May almighty God have mercy on us,
forgive us our sins,
and bring us to everlasting life.

R. Amen.

Hymn (No. 34)

+ Lord Jesus Christ, abide with us,
Now that the sun has run its course;
Let hope not be obscured by night,
But may faith's darkness be as light.

+ Lord Jesus Christ, grant us your peace,
And when the trials of earth shall cease;
Grant us the morning light of grace,
The radiant splendor of your face.

+ Immortal, Holy Threefold Light,
Yours be the kingdom, pow'r, and might;
All glory be eternally
To you, life giving Trinity.

Text: *Mane Nobiscum Domine*, paraphrased by Jerome
Leaman, 1967

Psalmody

Ant. Alleluia, alleluia, alleluia.

Book 1: Psalm 16
God is my portion, my inheritance

[SIT] + Preserve me, God, I take refuge in you.

THURSDAY IN EASTER SEASON
Night Prayer

I say to the Lord: "You are my God.
My happiness lies in you alone."

+ He has put into my heart a marvelous love
for the faithful ones who dwell in his land.
Those who choose other gods increase their
sorrows.
Never will I offer their offerings of blood.
Never will I take their name upon my lips.

+ O Lord, it is you who are my portion and cup;
it is you yourself who are my prize.
The lot marked out for me is my delight:
welcome indeed the heritage that falls to me!

+ I will bless the Lord who gives me counsel,
who even at night directs my heart.
I keep the Lord ever in my sight:
since he is at my right hand, I shall stand firm.

+ And so my heart rejoices, my soul is glad;
even my body shall rest in safety.
For you will not leave my soul among the dead,
nor let your beloved know decay.

+ You will show me the path of life,
the fullness of joy in your presence,
at your right hand happiness for ever.

[BOW] + Glory to the Father, and to the Son,
and to the Holy Spirit:

+ as it was in the beginning, is now,
and will be for ever. Amen.

Ant. Alleluia, alleluia, alleluia.

Reading: 1 Thessalonians 5: 23

May the God of peace make you perfect in
holiness. May he preserve you whole and entire,
spirit, soul, and body, irreproachable at the
coming of our Lord Jesus Christ.

Responsory

V. Into your hands, Lord, I commend
my spirit, alleluia, alleluia.

℟ Into your hands, Lord, I commend
my spirit, alleluia, alleluia.

℣ You have redeemed us, Lord God of truth.

℟ Alleluia, alleluia.

[Bow] ℣ Glory to the Father, and to the Son,
and to the Holy Spirit.

℟ Into your hands, Lord, I commend
my spirit, alleluia, alleluia.

The Nunc Dimittis

Ant. Protect us, Lord, as we stay awake; watch
[Stand] over us as we sleep, that awake, we may
keep watch with Christ, and asleep, rest in
his peace, alleluia.

Gospel Canticle: Luke 2: 29-32

✦ Lord, now you let your servant go in peace;
your word has been fulfilled:

✦ my own eyes have seen the salvation
which you have prepared in the sight
of every people:

✦ a light to reveal you to the nations
and the glory of your people Israel.

[Bow] ✦ Glory to the Father, and to the Son,
and to the Holy Spirit:

✦ as it was in the beginning, is now,

and will be for ever. Amen.

Ant. Protect us, Lord, as we stay awake; watch
over us as we sleep, that awake, we may keep
watch with Christ, and asleep, rest in his
peace, alleluia.

Prayer

Lord God,
send peaceful sleep
to refresh our tired bodies.
May your help always renew us
and keep us strong in your service.
We ask this through Christ our Lord.

℟ Amen.

Conclusion

✝ May the all-powerful Lord grant us a
restful night and a peaceful death.

℟ Amen.

Antiphon of the Blessed Virgin Mary

Queen of heaven, rejoice, alleluia.
The Son whom you merited to bear, alleluia,
has risen as he said, alleluia.
Pray to God for us, alleluia.

Rejoice and be glad, O Virgin Mary, alleluia.
For the Lord has truly risen, alleluia.

Introductory Rite

[Stand] V. God, ✠ come to my assistance.

R. Lord, make haste to help me.

[Bow] ✦ Glory to the Father, and to the Son,
and to the Holy Spirit:

✦ as it was in the beginning, is now,
and will be for ever. Amen, alleluia.

[A brief examination of conscience may be made]

Penitential Rite

I confess to almighty God,
and to you, my brothers and sisters,
that I have sinned through my own fault.

[strike breast]

in my thoughts and in my words,
in what I have done,
and in what I have failed to do;
and I ask blessed Mary, ever virgin,
all the angels and saints,
and you, my brothers and sisters,
to pray for me to the Lord our God.

V. May almighty God have mercy on us,
forgive us our sins,
and bring us to everlasting life.

R. Amen.

Hymn (No. 33)

✦ O Christ, you are the light and day
Which drives away the night,
The ever shining Sun of God
And pledge of future light.

✦ As now the ev'ning shadows fall
Please grant us, Lord, we pray,
A quiet night to rest in you
Until the break of day.

✦ Remember us, poor mortal men,
We humbly ask, O Lord,
And may your presence in our souls,
Be now our great reward.

Translator: Rev. M. Quinn, O.P. et al., 1965

Psalmody

Ant. Alleluia, alleluia, alleluia.

Book 3: Psalm 88
Prayer of a sick person

[Sit] ✦ Lord my God, I call for help by day;

FRIDAY IN EASTER SEASON
Night Prayer

I cry at night before you.
Let my prayer come into your presence.
O turn your ear to my cry.

✦ For my soul is filled with evils;
my life is on the brink of the grave.
I am reckoned as one in the tomb:
I have reached the end of my strength,

✦ like one alone among the dead;
like the slain lying in their graves;
like those you remember no more,
cut off, as they are, from your hand.

✦ You have laid me in the depths of the tomb,
in places that are dark, in the depths.
Your anger weighs down upon me:
I am drowned beneath your waves.

✦ You have taken away my friends
and made me hateful in their sight.
Imprisoned, I cannot escape;
my eyes are sunken with grief.

✦ I call to you, Lord, all the day long;
to you I stretch out my hands.
Will you work your wonders for the dead?
Will the shades stand and praise you?

✦ Will your love be told in the grave
or your faithfulness among the dead?
Will your wonders be known in the dark
or your justice in the land of oblivion?

✦ As for me, Lord, I call to you for help:
in the morning my prayer comes before you.
Lord, why do you reject me?
Why do you hide your face?

✦ Wretched, close to death from my youth,
I have borne your trials; I am numb.
Your fury has swept down upon me;
your terrors have utterly destroyed me.

✦ They surround me all the day like a flood,
they assail me all together.

Friend and neighbor you have taken away:
my one companion is darkness.

[Bow] ✦ Glory to the Father, and to the Son,
and to the Holy Spirit:
✦ as it was in the beginning, is now,
and will be for ever. Amen.

Ant. Alleluia, alleluia, alleluia.

Reading: Jeremiah 14: 9a

You are in our midst, O Lord,
your name we bear;
do not forsake us, O Lord, our God!

Responsory

℣. Into your hands, Lord, I commend
my spirit, alleluia, alleluia.

℟. Into your hands, Lord, I commend
my spirit, alleluia, alleluia.

℣. You have redeemed us, Lord God of truth.

℟. Alleluia, alleluia.

[Bow] ℣. Glory to the Father, and to the Son,
and to the Holy Spirit.

℟. Into your hands, Lord, I commend
my spirit, alleluia, alleluia.

The Nunc Dimittis

Ant. Protect us, Lord, as we stay awake; watch
[Stand] over us as we sleep, that awake, we may
keep watch with Christ, and asleep, rest in
his peace, alleluia.

Gospel Canticle: Luke 2: 29-32
✦ Lord, now you let your servant go in peace;
your word has been fulfilled:

✦ my own eyes have seen the salvation

which you have prepared in the sight
of every people:

✦ a light to reveal you to the nations
and the glory of your people Israel.

[Bow] ✦ Glory to the Father, and to the Son,
and to the Holy Spirit:
✦ as it was in the beginning, is now,
and will be for ever. Amen.

Ant. Protect us, Lord, as we stay awake; watch
over us as we sleep, that awake, we may keep
watch with Christ, and asleep, rest in his
peace, alleluia.

Prayer

All-powerful God,
keep us united with your Son
in his death and burial
so that we may rise to new life with him,
who lives and reigns for ever and ever.

℟. Amen.

Conclusion

✢ May the all-powerful Lord grant us a
restful night and a peaceful death.

℟. Amen.

Antiphon of the Blessed Virgin Mary

Queen of heaven, rejoice, alleluia.
The Son whom you merited to bear, alleluia,
has risen as he said, alleluia.
Pray to God for us, alleluia.

Rejoice and be glad, O Virgin Mary, alleluia.
For the Lord has truly risen, alleluia.

Introductory Rite

[Stand] V. God, ✠ come to my assistance.

R. Lord, make haste to help me.

[Bow] ✦ Glory to the Father, and to the Son,
and to the Holy Spirit:
✦ as it was in the beginning, is now,
and will be for ever. Amen, alleluia.

[A BRIEF EXAMINATION OF CONSCIENCE MAY BE MADE]

Penitential Rite

I confess to almighty God,
and to you, my brothers and sisters,
that I have sinned through my own fault.

[STRIKE BREAST]

in my thoughts and in my words,
in what I have done,
and in what I have failed to do;
and I ask blessed Mary, ever virgin,
all the angels and saints,
and you, my brothers and sisters,
to pray for me to the Lord our God.

V. May almighty God have mercy on us,
forgive us our sins,
and bring us to everlasting life.

R. Amen.

Hymn (No. 33)

✦ O Christ, you are the light and day
Which drives away the night,
The ever shining Sun of God
And pledge of future light.

✦ As now the ev'ning shadows fall
Please grant us, Lord, we pray,
A quiet night to rest in you
Until the break of day.

✦ Remember us, poor mortal men,
We humbly ask, O Lord,
And may your presence in our souls,
Be now our great reward.

Translator: Rev. M. Quinn, O.P. et al., 1965

Psalmody

Ant. 1   Alleluia, alleluia, alleluia.

Book 1: Psalm 4
Thanksgiving

[SIT] ✦ When I call, answer me, O God of justice;

SATURDAY IN EASTER SEASON
Night Prayer

from anguish you released me; have mercy
and hear me!

✦ O men, how long will your hearts be closed,
will you love what is futile and seek
what is false?

✦ It is the Lord who grants favors to those
whom he loves;
the Lord hears me whenever I call him.

✦ Fear him; do not sin: ponder on your bed
and be still.
Make justice your sacrifice and trust in the
Lord.

✦ "What can bring us happiness?" many say.
Let the light of your face shine on us, O Lord.

✦ You have put into my heart a greater joy
than they have from abundance of corn
and new wine.

✦ I will lie down in peace and sleep comes at once
for you alone, Lord, make me dwell in safety.

[Bow] ✦ Glory to the Father, and to the Son,
and to the Holy Spirit:
✦ as it was in the beginning, is now,
and will be for ever. Amen.

Book 5: Psalm 134
Evening prayer in the Temple

✦ O come, bless the Lord,
all you who serve the Lord,
who stand in the house of the Lord,
in the courts of the house of our God.

✦ Lift up your hands to the holy place
and bless the Lord through the night.

✦ May the Lord bless you from Zion,
he who made both heaven and earth.

[Bow] ✦ Glory to the Father, and to the Son,
and to the Holy Spirit:
✦ as it was in the beginning, is now,
and will be for ever. Amen.

Ant. Alleluia, alleluia, alleluia.

Reading: Deuteronomy 6: 4-7

Hear, O Israel! The Lord is our God, the Lord alone! Therefore, you shall love the Lord, your God, with all your heart, and with all your soul, and with all your strength. Take to heart these words which I enjoin on you today. Drill them into your children. Speak of them at home and abroad, whether you are busy or at rest.

Responsory

℣. Into your hands, Lord, I commend my spirit, alleluia, alleluia.

℟. Into your hands, Lord, I commend my spirit, alleluia, alleluia.

℣. You have redeemed us, Lord God of truth.

℟. Alleluia, alleluia.

[Bow] ℣. Glory to the Father, and to the Son, and to the Holy Spirit.

℟. Into your hands, Lord, I commend my spirit, alleluia, alleluia.

The Nunc Dimittis

Ant.
[Stand] Protect us, Lord, as we stay awake; watch over us as we sleep, that awake, we may keep watch with Christ, and asleep, rest in his peace, alleluia.

Gospel Canticle: Luke 2: 29-32

✦ Lord, now you let your servant go in peace; your word has been fulfilled:

✦ my own eyes have seen the salvation which you have prepared in the sight of every people:

✦ a light to reveal you to the nations and the glory of your people Israel.

[Bow] ✦ Glory to the Father, and to the Son, and to the Holy Spirit:

✦ as it was in the beginning, is now, and will be for ever. Amen.

Ant. Protect us, Lord, as we stay awake; watch over us as we sleep, that awake, we may keep watch with Christ, and asleep, rest in his peace, alleluia.

Prayer

Lord,
be with us throughout this night.
When day comes may we rise from sleep
to rejoice in the resurrection of your Christ,
who lives and reigns for ever and ever.

℟. Amen.

Conclusion

✠ May the all-powerful Lord grant us a restful night and a peaceful death.

℟. Amen.

Antiphon of the Blessed Virgin Mary

Queen of heaven, rejoice, alleluia.
The Son whom you merited to bear, alleluia,
has risen as he said, alleluia.
Pray to God for us, alleluia.

Rejoice and be glad, O Virgin Mary, alleluia.
For the Lord has truly risen, alleluia.

43

Introductory Rite

[STAND] V. God, ✠ come to my assistance.

℟. Lord, make haste to help me.

[BOW] ✦ Glory to the Father, and to the Son,
and to the Holy Spirit:

✦ as it was in the beginning, is now,
and will be for ever. Amen, alleluia.

[A BRIEF EXAMINATION OF CONSCIENCE MAY BE MADE]

Penitential Rite

I confess to almighty God,
and to you, my brothers and sisters,
that I have sinned through my own fault.

[STRIKE BREAST]

in my thoughts and in my words,
in what I have done,
and in what I have failed to do;
and I ask blessed Mary, ever virgin,
all the angels and saints,
and you, my brothers and sisters,
to pray for me to the Lord our God.

V. May almighty God have mercy on us,
forgive us our sins,
and bring us to everlasting life.

℟. Amen.

Hymn (No. 34)

✦ Lord Jesus Christ, abide with us,
Now that the sun has run its course;
Let hope not be obscured by night,
But may faith's darkness be as light.

✦ Lord Jesus Christ, grant us your peace,
And when the trials of earth shall cease;
Grant us the morning light of grace,
The radiant splendor of your face.

✦ Immortal, Holy Threefold Light,
Yours be the kingdom, pow'r, and might;
All glory be eternally
To you, life giving Trinity.

Text: *Mane Nobiscum Domine*, paraphrased by Jerome
Leaman, 1967

Psalmody

Ant. Alleluia, alleluia, alleluia.

SUNDAY IN EASTER SEASON
Night Prayer

Book 4: Psalm 91
Safe in God's sheltering care

[SIT] ✦ He who dwells in the shelter of the most High
and abides in the shade of the Almighty
says to the Lord "My refuge,
my stronghold, my God in whom in I trust!"

✦ It is he who will free you from the snare
of the fowler who seeks to destroy you;
he will conceal you with his pinions
and under his wings you will find refuge.

✦ You will not fear the terror of the night
nor the arrow that flies by day,
nor the plague that prowls in the darkness
nor the scourge that lays waste at noon.

✦ A thousand may fall at your side,
ten thousand fall at your right,
you, it will never approach;
his faithfulness is buckler and shield.

✦ Your eyes have only to look
to see how the wicked are repaid,
you who have said: "Lord, my refuge!"
and have made the Most High your dwelling.

✦ Upon you no evil shall fall,
no plague approach where you dwell.
For you has he commanded his angels,
to keep you in all your ways.

✦ They shall bear you upon their hands
lest you strike your foot against a stone.
On the lion and the viper you will tread
and trample the young lion and the dragon.

✦ Since he clings to me in love, I will free him;
protect him for he knows my name.
When he calls I shall answer: "I am with you."
I will save him in distress and give him glory.

✦ With length of life I will content him;
I shall let him see my saving power.

[Bow] ✢ Glory to the Father, and to the Son,
and to the Holy Spirit:
✢ as it was in the beginning, is now,
and will be for ever. Amen.

Ant. Alleluia, alleluia, alleluia.

Reading: Revelation 22: 4-5

They shall see him face to face and bear his name on their foreheads. The night shall be no more. They will need no light from lamps or the sun, for the Lord God shall give them light, and they shall reign forever.

Responsory

℣. Into your hands, Lord, I commend
my spirit, alleluia, alleluia.

℟. Into your hands, Lord, I commend
my spirit, alleluia, alleluia.

℣. You have redeemed us, Lord God of truth.

℟. Alleluia, alleluia.

[Bow] ℣. Glory to the Father, and to the Son,
and to the Holy Spirit.

℟. Into your hands, Lord, I commend
my spirit, alleluia, alleluia.

The Nunc Dimittis

Ant.
[Stand] Protect us, Lord, as we stay awake; watch over us as we sleep, that awake, we may keep watch with Christ, and asleep, rest in his peace, alleluia.

Gospel Canticle: Luke 2: 29-32

✢ Lord, now you let your servant go in peace; your word has been fulfilled:

✢ my own eyes have seen the salvation which you have prepared in the sight of every people:

✢ a light to reveal you to the nations and the glory of your people Israel.

[Bow] ✢ Glory to the Father, and to the Son,
and to the Holy Spirit:
✢ as it was in the beginning, is now,
and will be for ever. Amen.

Ant. Protect us, Lord, as we stay awake; watch over us as we sleep, that awake, we may keep watch with Christ, and asleep, rest in his peace, alleluia.

Prayer

Lord,
we have celebrated today
the mystery of the rising of Christ to new life.
May we now rest in your peace,
safe from all that could harm us,
and rise again refreshed and joyful,
to praise you throughout another day.
We ask this through Christ our Lord.

℟ Amen.

Conclusion

✢ May the all-powerful Lord grant us a restful night and a peaceful death.

℟ Amen.

Antiphon of the Blessed Virgin Mary

Queen of heaven, rejoice, alleluia.
The Son whom you merited
   to bear, alleluia,
has risen as he said, alleluia.
Pray to God for us, alleluia.

Rejoice and be glad,
   O Virgin Mary, alleluia.
For the Lord has truly risen, alleluia.

Solemnities

Special Feasts Observed
in the Universal Church

Introductory Rite

[STAND] V. God, ✠ come to my assistance.

R. Lord, make haste to help me.

[BOW] ✦ Glory to the Father, and to the Son,
and to the Holy Spirit:

✦ as it was in the beginning, is now,
and will be for ever. Amen (alleluia).

[A BRIEF EXAMINATION OF CONSCIENCE MAY BE MADE]

Penitential Rite

I confess to almighty God,
and to you, my brothers and sisters,
that I have sinned through my own fault.

[STRIKE BREAST]

in my thoughts and in my words,
in what I have done,
and in what I have failed to do;
and I ask blessed Mary, ever virgin,
all the angels and saints,
and you, my brothers and sisters,
to pray for me to the Lord our God.

V. May almighty God have mercy on us,
forgive us our sins,
and bring us to everlasting life.

R. Amen.

Hymn (No. 33)

✦ O Christ, you are the light and day
Which drives away the night,
The ever shining Sun of God
And pledge of future light.

✦ As now the ev'ning shadows fall
Please grant us, Lord, we pray,
A quiet night to rest in you
Until the break of day.

✦ Remember us, poor mortal men,
We humbly ask, O Lord,
And may your presence in our souls,
Be now our great reward.

Translator: Rev. M. Quinn, O.P. et al., 1965

Psalmody

Ant. 1 Have mercy, Lord, and hear my prayer.

Book 1: Psalm 4
Thanksgiving

[SIT] ✦ When I call, answer me, O God of justice;

SOLEMNITY VIGIL
Night Prayer
REGULAR SEASON

from anguish you released me; have mercy
and hear me!

✦ O men, how long will your hearts be closed,
will you love what is futile and seek what is false?

✦ It is the Lord who grants favors to those
whom he loves;
the Lord hears me whenever I call him.

✦ Fear him; do not sin: ponder on your bed
and be still.
Make justice your sacrifice and trust in the Lord.

✦ "What can bring us happiness?" many say.
Let the light of your face shine on us, O Lord.

✦ You have put into my heart a greater joy
than they have from abundance of corn
and new wine.

✦ I will lie down in peace and sleep comes at once
for you alone, Lord, make me dwell in safety.

[BOW] ✦ Glory to the Father, and to the Son,
and to the Holy Spirit:

✦ as it was in the beginning, is now,
and will be for ever. Amen.

Ant. Have mercy, Lord, and hear my prayer.

Ant. 2 In the silent hours of night, bless the Lord.

Book 5: Psalm 134
Evening prayer in the Temple

✦ O come, bless the Lord,
all you who serve the Lord,
who stand in the house of the Lord,
in the courts of the house of our God.

✦ Lift up your hands to the holy place
and bless the Lord through the night.

✦ May the Lord bless you from Zion,
he who made both heaven and earth.

[BOW] ✦ Glory to the Father, and to the Son,
and to the Holy Spirit:

✦ as it was in the beginning, is now,
and will be for ever. Amen.

Ant.   In the silent hours of night, bless the Lord.

Reading: Deuteronomy 6: 4-7

Hear, O Israel! The Lord is our God, the Lord alone! Therefore, you shall love the Lord, your God, with all your heart, and with all your soul, and with all your strength. Take to heart these words which I enjoin on you today. Drill them into your children. Speak of them at home and abroad, whether you are busy or at rest.

Responsory

℣. Into your hands, Lord, I commend my spirit.

℟. Into your hands, Lord, I commend my spirit.

℣. You have redeemed us, Lord God of truth.

℟. I commend my spitit.

[Bow] ℣. Glory to the Father, and to the Son, and to the Holy Spirit.

℟. Into your hands, Lord, I commend my spirit.

The Nunc Dimittis

Ant.
[Stand]   Protect us, Lord, as we stay awake; watch over us as we sleep, that awake, we may keep watch with Christ, and asleep, rest in his peace (alleluia).

Gospel Canticle: Luke 2: 29-32

✢ Lord, now you let your servant go in peace; your word has been fulfilled:

✢ my own eyes have seen the salvation which you have prepared in the sight of every people:

✢ a light to reveal you to the nations and the glory of your people Israel.

[Bow] ✢ Glory to the Father, and to the Son,

and to the Holy Spirit:

✢ as it was in the beginning, is now, and will be for ever. Amen.

Ant.   Protect us, Lord, as we stay awake; watch over us as we sleep, that awake, we may keep watch with Christ, and asleep, rest in his peace (alleluia).

Prayer

Lord,
we beg you to visit this house
and banish from it
all the deadly power of the enemy.
May your holy angels dwell here
to keep us in peace,
and may your blessing be upon us always.
We ask this through Christ our Lord.

℟ Amen.

Conclusion

✢ May the all-powerful Lord grant us a restful night and a peaceful death.

℟ Amen.

Antiphon of the Blessed Virgin Mary

[See back flap for Advent antiphon]

Hail, holy Queen, mother of mercy,
our life, our sweetness, and our hope.
To you do we cry,
poor banished children of Eve.
To you do we send up our sighs,
mourning and weeping in this vale of tears.
Turn then, most gracious advocate,
your eyes of mercy toward us,
and after this exile
show us the blessed fruit of
    your womb, Jesus.
O clement, O loving,
O sweet Virgin Mary.

Introductory Rite

[STAND] V. God, ☩ come to my assistance.

R. Lord, make haste to help me.

[BOW] • Glory to the Father, and to the Son,
and to the Holy Spirit:
• as it was in the beginning, is now,
and will be for ever. Amen (alleluia).

[A BRIEF EXAMINATION OF CONSCIENCE MAY BE MADE]

Penitential Rite

I confess to almighty God,
and to you, my brothers and sisters,
that I have sinned through my own fault.

[STRIKE BREAST]

in my thoughts and in my words,
in what I have done,
and in what I have failed to do;
and I ask blessed Mary, ever virgin,
all the angels and saints,
and you, my brothers and sisters,
to pray for me to the Lord our God.

V. May almighty God have mercy on us,
forgive us our sins,
and bring us to everlasting life.

R. Amen.

Hymn (No. 34)

• Lord Jesus Christ, abide with us,
Now that the sun has run its course;
Let hope not be obscured by night,
But may faith's darkness be as light.

• Lord Jesus Christ, grant us your peace,
And when the trials of earth shall cease;
Grant us the morning light of grace,
The radiant splendor of your face.

• Immortal, Holy Threefold Light,
Yours be the kingdom, pow'r, and might;
All glory be eternally
To you, life giving Trinity.

Text: *Mane Nobiscum Domine,* paraphrased by Jerome
Leaman, 1967

Psalmody

Ant. Night holds no terrors for me sleeping
under God's wings.

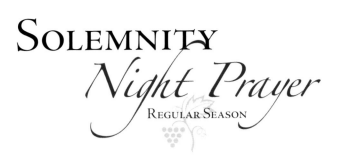

SOLEMNITY
Night Prayer
REGULAR SEASON

Book 4: Psalm 91

Safe in God's sheltering care

[SIT] • He who dwells in the shelter of the most High
and abides in the shade of the Almighty
says to the Lord "My refuge,
my stronghold, my God in whom in I trust!"

• It is he who will free you from the snare
of the fowler who seeks to destroy you;
he will conceal you with his pinions
and under his wings you will find refuge.

• You will not fear the terror of the night
nor the arrow that flies by day,
nor the plague that prowls in the darkness
nor the scourge that lays waste at noon.

• A thousand may fall at your side,
ten thousand fall at your right,
you, it will never approach;
his faithfulness is buckler and shield.

• Your eyes have only to look
to see how the wicked are repaid,
you who have said: "Lord, my refuge!"
and have made the Most High your dwelling.

• Upon you no evil shall fall,
no plague approach where you dwell.
For you has he commanded his angels,
to keep you in all your ways.

• They shall bear you upon their hands
lest you strike your foot against a stone.
On the lion and the viper you will tread
and trample the young lion and the dragon.

• Since he clings to me in love, I will free him;
protect him for he knows my name.
When he calls I shall answer: "I am with you."
I will save him in distress and give him glory.

• With length of life I will content him;
I shall let him see my saving power.

[BOW] • Glory to the Father, and to the Son,
and to the Holy Spirit:

+ as it was in the beginning, is now,
and will be for ever. Amen.

Ant. Night holds no terrors for me sleeping under God's wings.

Reading: Revelation 22: 4-5

They shall see him face to face and bear his name on their foreheads. The night shall be no more. They will need no light from lamps or the sun, for the Lord God shall give them light, and they shall reign forever.

Responsory

℣. Into your hands, Lord, I commend my spirit.

℟. Into your hands, Lord, I commend my spirit.

℣. You have redeemed us, Lord God of truth.

℟. I commend my spirit.

[Bow] ℣. Glory to the Father, and to the Son, and to the Holy Spirit.

℟. Into your hands, Lord, I commend my spirit.

The Nunc Dimittis

Ant.
[Stand] Protect us, Lord, as we stay awake; watch over us as we sleep, that awake, we may keep watch with Christ, and asleep, rest in his peace (alleluia).

Gospel Canticle: Luke 2: 29-32

+ Lord, now you let your servant go in peace; your word has been fulfilled:

+ my own eyes have seen the salvation which you have prepared in the sight of every people:

+ a light to reveal you to the nations and the glory of your people Israel.

[Bow] + Glory to the Father, and to the Son,

and to the Holy Spirit:

+ as it was in the beginning, is now, and will be for ever. Amen.

Ant. Protect us, Lord, as we stay awake; watch over us as we sleep, that awake, we may keep watch with Christ, and asleep, rest in his peace (alleluia).

Prayer

Lord,
we beg you to visit this house
and banish from it
all the deadly power of the enemy.
May your holy angels dwell here
to keep us in peace,
and may your blessing be upon us always.
We ask this through Christ our Lord.

℟. Amen.

Conclusion

+ May the all-powerful Lord grant us a restful night and a peaceful death.

℟. Amen.

Antiphon of the Blessed Virgin Mary

[See back flap for Advent antiphon]

Hail, holy Queen, mother of mercy,
our life, our sweetness, and our hope.
To you do we cry,
poor banished children of Eve.
To you do we send up our sighs,
mourning and weeping in this vale of tears.
Turn then, most gracious advocate,
your eyes of mercy toward us,
and after this exile
show us the blessed fruit of
    your womb, Jesus.
O clement, O loving,
O sweet Virgin Mary.

51

Introductory Rite

[Stand] V. God, ✠ come to my assistance.

R. Lord, make haste to help me.

[Bow] + Glory to the Father, and to the Son,
and to the Holy Spirit:

+ as it was in the beginning, is now,
and will be for ever. Amen (alleluia).

[A brief examination of conscience may be made]

Penitential Rite

I confess to almighty God,
and to you, my brothers and sisters,
that I have sinned through my own fault.

[strike breast]

in my thoughts and in my words,
in what I have done,
and in what I have failed to do;
and I ask blessed Mary, ever virgin,
all the angels and saints,
and you, my brothers and sisters,
to pray for me to the Lord our God.

V. May almighty God have mercy on us,
forgive us our sins,
and bring us to everlasting life.

R. Amen.

Hymn (No. 33)

+ O Christ, you are the light and day
Which drives away the night,
The ever shining Sun of God
And pledge of future light.

+ As now the ev'ning shadows fall
Please grant us, Lord, we pray,
A quiet night to rest in you
Until the break of day.

+ Remember us, poor mortal men,
We humbly ask, O Lord,
And may your presence in our souls,
Be now our great reward.

Translator: Rev. M. Quinn, O.P. et al., 1965

Psalmody

Ant. 1 Alleluia, alleluia, alleluia.

Book 1: Psalm 4
Thanksgiving

[Sit] + When I call, answer me, O God of justice;

from anguish you released me; have mercy
and hear me!

+ O men, how long will your hearts be closed,
will you love what is futile and seek
what is false?

+ It is the Lord who grants favors to those
whom he loves;
the Lord hears me whenever I call him.

+ Fear him; do not sin: ponder on your bed
and be still.
Make justice your sacrifice and trust
in the Lord.

+ "What can bring us happiness?" many say.
Let the light of your face shine on us, O Lord.

+ You have put into my heart a greater joy
than they have from abundance of corn
and new wine.

+ I will lie down in peace and sleep comes at once
for you alone, Lord, make me dwell in safety.

[Bow] + Glory to the Father, and to the Son,
and to the Holy Spirit:

+ as it was in the beginning, is now,
and will be for ever. Amen.

Book 5: Psalm 134
Evening prayer in the Temple

+ O come, bless the Lord,
all you who serve the Lord,
who stand in the house of the Lord,
in the courts of the house of our God.

+ Lift up your hands to the holy place
and bless the Lord through the night.

+ May the Lord bless you from Zion,
he who made both heaven and earth.

[Bow] + Glory to the Father, and to the Son,
and to the Holy Spirit:

+ as it was in the beginning, is now,
and will be for ever. Amen.

Ant.   Alleluia, alleluia, alleluia.

Reading: Deuteronomy 6: 4-7

Hear, O Israel! The Lord is our God, the Lord alone! Therefore, you shall love the Lord, your God, with all your heart, and with all your soul, and with all your strength. Take to heart these words which I enjoin on you today. Drill them into your children. Speak of them at home and abroad, whether you are busy or at rest.

If the solemnity occurs during the octave of Easter (within eight days of Easter Sunday) the following antiphon is recited instead of the Responsory "Into your hands."

Ant.   This is the day the Lord has made; let us rejoice and be glad, alleluia.

Responsory

℣. Into your hands, Lord, I commend my spirit, alleluia, alleluia.

℟. Into your hands, Lord, I commend my spirit, alleluia, alleluia.

℣. You have redeemed us, Lord God of truth.

℟. Alleluia, alleluia.

[Bow] ℣. Glory to the Father, and to the Son, and to the Holy Spirit.

℟. Into your hands, Lord, I commend my spirit, alleluia, alleluia.

The Nunc Dimittis

Ant.   Protect us, Lord, as we stay awake; watch
[Stand]   over us as we sleep, that awake, we may keep watch with Christ, and asleep, rest in his peace, alleluia.

Gospel Canticle: Luke 2: 29-32

✦Lord, now you let your servant go in peace; your word has been fulfilled:

✦my own eyes have seen the salvation which you have prepared in the sight of every people:

✦a light to reveal you to the nations and the glory of your people Israel.

[Bow] ✦Glory to the Father, and to the Son, and to the Holy Spirit:

✦as it was in the beginning, is now, and will be for ever. Amen.

Ant.   Protect us, Lord, as we stay awake; watch over us as we sleep, that awake, we may keep watch with Christ, and asleep, rest in his peace, alleluia.

Prayer *(During the octave of Easter)*

Lord,
be with us throughout this night.
When day comes may we rise from sleep
to rejoice in the resurrection of
    your Christ,
who lives and reigns for ever and ever.

Prayer *(During the Easter Season, but not the octave.)*

Lord,
we beg you to visit this house
and banish from it
all the deadly power of the enemy.
May your holy angels dwell here
to keep us in peace,
and may your blessing be upon us always.
We ask this through Christ our Lord.

℟ Amen.

Conclusion

✠ May the all-powerful Lord grant us a restful night and a peaceful death.

℟ Amen.

Antiphon of the Blessed Virgin Mary

Queen of heaven, rejoice, alleluia.
The Son whom you merited
    to bear, alleluia,
has risen as he said, alleluia.
Pray to God for us, alleluia.

Rejoice and be glad,
    O Virgin Mary, alleluia.
For the Lord has truly risen, alleluia.

53

Introductory Rite

[STAND] V. God, ✠ come to my assistance.
  R. Lord, make haste to help me.

[BOW] ✦ Glory to the Father, and to the Son,
    and to the Holy Spirit:
  ✦ as it was in the beginning, is now,
    and will be for ever. Amen (alleluia).

[A BRIEF EXAMINATION OF CONSCIENCE MAY BE MADE]

Penitential Rite

I confess to almighty God,
and to you, my brothers and sisters,
that I have sinned through my own fault.

[STRIKE BREAST]

in my thoughts and in my words,
in what I have done,
and in what I have failed to do;
and I ask blessed Mary, ever virgin,
all the angels and saints,
and you, my brothers and sisters,
to pray for me to the Lord our God.

V. May almighty God have mercy on us,
  forgive us our sins,
  and bring us to everlasting life.

R. Amen.

Hymn (No. 34)

✦ Lord Jesus Christ, abide with us,
  Now that the sun has run its course;
  Let hope not be obscured by night,
  But may faith's darkness be as light.

✦ Lord Jesus Christ, grant us your peace,
  And when the trials of earth shall cease;
  Grant us the morning light of grace,
  The radiant splendor of your face.

✦ Immortal, Holy Threefold Light,
  Yours be the kingdom, pow'r, and might;
  All glory be eternally
  To you, life giving Trinity.

Text: *Mane Nobiscum Domine*, paraphrased by Jerome
Leaman, 1967

Psalmody

Ant. Alleluia, alleluia, alleluia.

SOLEMNITY
Night Prayer
EASTER SEASON

Book 4: Psalm 91
Safe in God's sheltering care

[SIT] ✦ He who dwells in the shelter of the most High
  and abides in the shade of the Almighty
  says to the Lord "My refuge,
  my stronghold, my God in whom in I trust!"

✦ It is he who will free you from the snare
  of the fowler who seeks to destroy you;
  he will conceal you with his pinions
  and under his wings you will find refuge.

✦ You will not fear the terror of the night
  nor the arrow that flies by day,
  nor the plague that prowls in the darkness
  nor the scourge that lays waste at noon.

✦ A thousand may fall at your side,
  ten thousand fall at your right,
  you, it will never approach;
  his faithfulness is buckler and shield.

✦ Your eyes have only to look
  to see how the wicked are repaid,
  you who have said: "Lord, my refuge!"
  and have made the Most High your dwelling.

✦ Upon you no evil shall fall,
  no plague approach where you dwell.
  For you has he commanded his angels,
  to keep you in all your ways.

✦ They shall bear you upon their hands
  lest you strike your foot against a stone.
  On the lion and the viper you will tread
  and trample the young lion and the dragon.

✦ Since he clings to me in love, I will free him;
  protect him for he knows my name.
  When he calls I shall answer: "I am with you."
  I will save him in distress and give him glory.

✦ With length of life I will content him;
  I shall let him see my saving power.

[Bow] ✦ Glory to the Father, and to the Son,
and to the Holy Spirit:
✦ as it was in the beginning, is now,
and will be for ever. Amen.

Ant. Alleluia, alleluia, alleluia.

Reading: Revelation 22: 4-5

They shall see him face to face and bear
his name on their foreheads. The night
shall be no more. They will need no light
from lamps or the sun, for the Lord God
shall give them light, and they shall reign
forever.

If the solemnity occurs during the octave of Easter (within
eight days of Easter Sunday) the following antiphon is
recited instead of the Responsory "Into your hands."

Ant. This is the day the Lord has made; let us
rejoice and be glad, alleluia.

Responsory

℣. Into your hands, Lord, I commend
my spirit, alleluia, alleluia.
℟. Into your hands, Lord, I commend
my spirit, alleluia, alleluia.
℣. You have redeemed us, Lord God of truth.
℟. Alleluia, alleluia.
[Bow] ℣. Glory to the Father, and to the Son,
and to the Holy Spirit.
℟. Into your hands, Lord, I commend
my spirit, alleluia, alleluia.

The Nunc Dimittis

Ant. Protect us, Lord, as we stay awake; watch
[Stand] over us as we sleep, that awake, we may
keep watch with Christ, and asleep, rest in
his peace, alleluia.

Gospel Canticle: Luke 2: 29-32

✦ Lord, now you let your servant go in peace;
your word has been fulfilled:

✦ my own eyes have seen the salvation
which you have prepared in the sight
of every people:

✦ a light to reveal you to the nations
and the glory of your people Israel.

[Bow] ✦ Glory to the Father, and to the Son,
and to the Holy Spirit:
✦ as it was in the beginning, is now,
and will be for ever. Amen.

Ant. Protect us, Lord, as we stay awake; watch
over us as we sleep, that awake, we may keep
watch with Christ, and asleep, rest in his
peace, alleluia.

Prayer (During the octave of Easter)

Lord,
we have celebrated today
the mystery of the rising of Christ to new life.
May we now rest in your peace,
safe from all that could harm us,
and rise again refreshed and joyful,
to praise you throughout another day.
We ask this through Christ our Lord.

℟ Amen.

Prayer (During the Easter Season, but not the octave.)

Lord,
we beg you to visit this house
and banish from it
all the deadly power of the enemy.
May your holy angels dwell here
to keep us in peace,
and may your blessing be upon us always.
We ask this through Christ our Lord.

℟ Amen.

Conclusion

✠ May the all-powerful Lord grant us a
restful night and a peaceful death.
℟ Amen.

Antiphon of the Blessed Virgin Mary

Queen of heaven, rejoice, alleluia.
The Son whom you merited to bear, alleluia,
has risen as he said, alleluia.
Pray to God for us, alleluia.

Rejoice and be glad, O Virgin Mary, alleluia.
For the Lord has truly risen, alleluia.

LITURGICAL CALENDAR

The calendar on the following pages indicates the feast to be observed for any night of the year through 2016. To find the correct feast, locate the *current year*; then, the *month and date*; and finally the *page number* for that feast or current season.

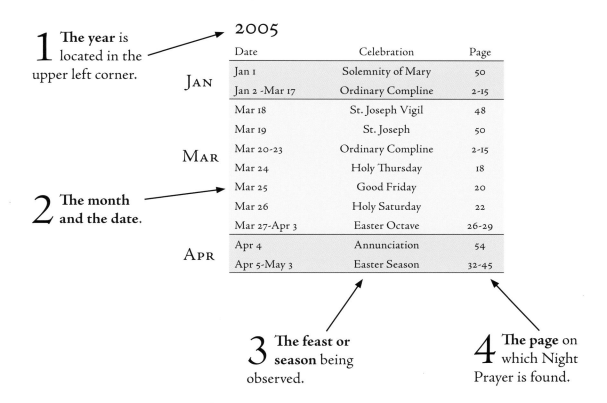

1 **The year** is located in the upper left corner.

2 **The month** and **the date**.

2005

Date	Celebration	Page
Jan 1	Solemnity of Mary	50
Jan 2 -Mar 17	Ordinary Compline	2-15
Mar 18	St. Joseph Vigil	48
Mar 19	St. Joseph	50
Mar 20-23	Ordinary Compline	2-15
Mar 24	Holy Thursday	18
Mar 25	Good Friday	20
Mar 26	Holy Saturday	22
Mar 27-Apr 3	Easter Octave	26-29
Apr 4	Annunciation	54
Apr 5-May 3	Easter Season	32-45

JAN

MAR

APR

3 **The feast or season** being observed.

4 **The page** on which Night Prayer is found.

SPECIAL NOTE REGARDING SOLEMNITIES

At times a solemnity will not appear on the Liturgical Calendar. If a solemnity falls on a Sunday (for example, Pentecost), or is moved to a Sunday (for example, the Ephiphany), then ordinary Sunday Night Prayer is prayed, as indicated by the calendar.

Liturgical Calendar

2005

	Date	Celebration	Page
Jan	Jan 1	Solemnity of Mary	50
	Jan 2 -Mar 17	Ordinary Compline	2-15
Mar	Mar 18	St. Joseph Vigil	48
	Mar 19	St. Joseph	50
	Mar 20-23	Ordinary Compline	2-15
	Mar 24	Holy Thursday	18
	Mar 25	Good Friday	20
	Mar 26	Holy Saturday	22
	Mar 27-Apr 3	Easter Octave	26-29
Apr	Apr 4	Annunciation	54
	Apr 5-May 3	Easter Season	32-45
	May 4	Ascension Vigil	52
May	May 5	Ascension	54
	May 6-15	Easter Season	32-45
	May 16-Jun 1	Ordinary Compline	2-15
	Jun 2	Most Sacr. Heart Vigil	48
	Jun 3	Sacred Heart	50
	Jun 4-22	Ordinary Compline	2-15
June	Jun 23	St. John Bapt. Vigil	48
	Jun 24	St. John the Baptist	50
	Jun 25-27	Ordinary Compline	2-15
	Jun 28	Sts. Peter & Paul Vigil	48
	Jun 29	Sts. Peter & Paul	50
	Jun 30-Aug 14	Ordinary Compline	2-15
Aug	Aug 15	Assumption of Mary	50
	Aug 16-Oct 30	Ordinary Compline	2-15
Oct	Oct 31	All Saints Vigil	48
Nov	Nov 1	All Saints	50
	Nov 2-Dec 6	Ordinary Compline	2-15
	Dec 7	Imm Conception Vigil	48
Dec	Dec 8	Immaculate Conception	50
	Dec 9-Dec 31	Ordinary Compline	2-15

2006

	Date	Celebration	Page
Jan	Jan 1-Mar 23	Ordinary Compline	2-15
Mar	Mar 24	Annunciation Vigil	48
	Mar 25	Annunciation	50
	Mar 26-Apr 12	Ordinary Compline	2-15
	Apr 13	Holy Thursday	18
Apr	Apr 14	Good Friday	20
	Apr 15	Holy Saturday	22
	Apr 16-23	Easter Octave	26-29
	Apr 24-May 23	Easter Season	32-45
May	May 24	Ascension Vigil	52
	May 25	Ascension	54
	May 26-Jun 4	Easter Season	32-45
	Jun 5-21	Ordinary Compline	2-15
	Jun 22	Most Sacr. Heart Vigil	48
	Jun 23	Sacred Heart	50
June	Jun 24	St. John Bapt.	50
	Jun 25-27	Ordinary Compline	2-15
	Jun 28	Sts. Peter & Paul Vigil	48
	Jun 29	Sts. Peter & Paul	50
	Jun 30-Aug 13	Ordinary Compline	2-15
Aug	Aug 14	Assumption Vigil	48
	Aug 15	Assumption of Mary	50
	Aug 16-Oct 30	Ordinary Compline	2-15
Oct	Oct 31	All Saints Vigil	48
Nov	Nov 1	All Saints	50
	Nov 2-Dec 6	Ordinary Compline	2-15
	Dec 7	Imm Conception Vigil	48
	Dec 8	Immaculate Conception	50
Dec	Dec 9-Dec 23	Ordinary Compline	2-15
	Dec 24	Christmas Vigil	48
	Dec 25	Christmas	50
	Dec 26-Dec 31	Ordinary Compline	2-15

Liturgical Calendar

2007

	Date	Celebration	Page
Jan	Jan 1	Solemnity of Mary	50
	Jan 2 -Mar 18	Ordinary Compline	2-15
Mar	Mar 19	St. Joseph	50
	Mar 20-Apr 4	Ordinary Compline	2-15
Apr	Apr 5	Holy Thursday	18
	Apr 6	Good Friday	20
	Apr 7	Holy Saturday	22
	Apr 8-15	Easter Octave	26-29
	Apr 16-May 15	Easter Season	32-45
May	May 16	Ascension Vigil	52
	May 17	Ascension	54
	May 18-27	Easter Season	32-45
	May 28-Jun 13	Ordinary Compline	2-15
June	Jun 14	Most Sacr. Heart Vigil	48
	Jun 15	Sacred Heart	50
	Jun 16-27	Ordinary Compline	2-15
	Jun 28	Sts. Peter & Paul Vigil	48
	Jun 29	Sts. Peter & Paul	50
	Jun 30-Aug 13	Ordinary Compline	2-15
Aug	Aug 14	Assumption Vigil	48
	Aug 15	Assumption of Mary	50
	Aug 16-Oct 30	Ordinary Compline	2-15
Oct	Oct 31	All Saints Vigil	48
Nov	Nov 1	All Saints	50
	Nov 2-Dec 6	Ordinary Compline	2-15
	Dec 7	Imm Conception Vigil	48
	Dec 8	Immaculate Conception	50
Dec	Dec 9-Dec 23	Ordinary Compline	2-15
	Dec 24	Christmas Vigil	48
	Dec 25	Christmas	50
	Dec 26-Dec 30	Ordinary Compline	2-15
	Dec 31	Sol. of Mary Vigil	48

2008

	Date	Celebration	Page
Jan	Jan 1	Solemnity of Mary	50
	Jan 2 -Mar 19	Ordinary Compline	2-15
Mar	Mar 20	Holy Thursday	18
	Mar 21	Good Friday	20
	Mar 22	Holy Saturday	22
	Mar 23-30	Easter Octave	26-29
	Mar 31	St. Joseph	54
Apr	Apr 1	Annunciation	54
	Apr 2-29	Easter Season	32-45
	Apr 30	Ascension Vigil	52
May	May 1	Ascension	54
	May 2-11	Easter Season	32-45
	May 12-28	Ordinary Compline	2-15
	May 29	Most Sacr. Heart Vigil	48
	May 30	Sacred Heart	50
	May 31-Jun 22	Ordinary Compline	2-15
	Jun 23	St. John Bapt. Vigil	48
June	Jun 24	St. John the Baptist	50
	Jun 25-Aug 13	Ordinary Compline	2-15
	Aug 14	Assumption Vigil	48
Aug	Aug 15	Assumption of Mary	50
	Aug 16-Oct 30	Ordinary Compline	2-15
Oct	Oct 31	All Saints Vigil	48
Nov	Nov 1	All Saints	50
	Nov 2-Dec 7	Ordinary Compline	2-15
	Dec 8	Immaculate Conception	50
	Dec 9-Dec 23	Ordinary Compline	2-15
Dec	Dec 24	Christmas Vigil	48
	Dec 25	Christmas	50
	Dec 26-Dec 30	Ordinary Compline	2-15
	Dec 31	Sol. of Mary Vigil	48

Liturgical Calendar

2009

	Date	Celebration	Page
Jan	Jan 1	Solemnity of Mary	50
	Jan 2 -Mar 17	Ordinary Compline	2-15
	Mar 18	St. Joseph Vigil	48
	Mar 19	St. Joseph	50
Mar	Mar 20-23	Ordinary Compline	2-15
	Mar 24	Annunciation Vigil	48
	Mar 25	Annunciation	50
	Mar 26-Apr 8	Ordinary Compline	2-15
	Apr 9	Holy Thursday	18
	Apr 10	Good Friday	20
Apr	Apr 11	Holy Saturday	22
	Apr 12-19	Easter Octave	26-29
	Apr 20-May 19	Easter Season	32-45
	May 20	Ascension Vigil	52
May	May 21	Ascension	54
	May 22-31	Easter Season	32-45
	Jun 1-17	Ordinary Compline	2-15
	Jun 18	Most Sacr. Heart Vigil	48
	Jun 19	Sacred Heart	50
June	Jun 20-22	Ordinary Compline	2-15
	Jun 23	St. John Bapt. Vigil	48
	Jun 24	St. John the Baptist	50
	Jun 25-28	Ordinary Compline	2-15
	Jun 29	Sts. Peter & Paul	50
	Jun 30-Aug 13	Ordinary Compline	2-15
	Aug 14	Assumption Vigil	48
Aug	Aug 15	Assumption of Mary	50
	Aug 16-Dec 6	Ordinary Compline	2-15
	Dec 7	Imm Conception Vigil	48
	Dec 8	Immaculate Conception	50
	Dec 9-Dec 23	Ordinary Compline	2-15
Dec	Dec 24	Christmas Vigil	48
	Dec 25	Christmas	50
	Dec 26-30	Ordinary Compline	2-15
	Dec 31	Sol. of Mary Vigil	48

2010

	Date	Celebration	Page
Jan	Jan 1	Solemnity of Mary	50
	Jan 2-Mar 17	Ordinary Compline	2-15
	Mar 18	St. Joseph Vigil	48
	Mar 19	St. Joseph	50
Mar	Mar 20-23	Ordinary Compline	2-15
	Mar 24	Annunciation Vigil	48
	Mar 25	Annunciation	50
	Mar 26-31	Ordinary Compline	2-15
	Apr 1	Holy Thursday	18
	Apr 2	Good Friday	20
Apr	Apr 3	Holy Saturday	22
	Apr 4-11	Easter Octave	26-29
	Apr 12-May 11	Easter Season	32-45
	May 12	Ascension Vigil	52
May	May 13	Ascension	54
	May 14-23	Easter Season	32-45
	May 23-Jun 9	Ordinary Compline	2-15
	Jun 10	Most Sacr. Heart Vigil	48
	Jun 11	Sacred Heart	50
	Jun 12-22	Ordinary Compline	2-15
	Jun 23	St. John Bapt. Vigil	48
June	Jun 24	St. John Bapt.	50
	Jun 25-27	Ordinary Compline	2-15
	Jun 28	Sts. Peter & Paul Vigil	48
	Jun 29	Sts. Peter & Paul	50
	Jun 30-Oct 31	Ordinary Compline	2-15
Nov	Nov 1	All Saints	50
	Nov 2-Dec 6	Ordinary Compline	2-15
	Dec 7	Imm Conception Vigil	48
	Dec 8	Immaculate Conception	50
	Dec 9-Dec 23	Ordinary Compline	2-15
Dec	Dec 24	Christmas Vigil	48
	Dec 25	Christmas	50
	Dec 26-Dec 30	Ordinary Compline	2-15
	Dec 31	Sol. of Mary Vigil	48

Liturgical Calendar

2011

	Date	Celebration	Page
Jan	Jan 1	Solemnity of Mary	50
	Jan 2 -Mar 17	Ordinary Compline	2-15
	Mar 18	St. Joseph Vigil	48
	Mar 19	St. Joseph	50
Mar	Mar 20-23	Ordinary Compline	2-15
	Mar 24	Annunciation Vigil	48
	Mar 25	Annunciation	50
	Mar 26-Apr 20	Ordinary Compline	2-15
	Apr 21	Holy Thursday	18
	Apr 22	Good Friday	20
Apr	Apr 23	Holy Saturday	22
	Apr 24-May 1	Easter Octave	26-29
May	May 1-31	Easter Season	32-45
	Jun 1	Ascension Vigil	52
	Jun 2	Ascension	54
	Jun 3-12	Easter Season	32-45
June	Jun 13-22	Ordinary Compline	2-15
	Jun 23	St. John Bapt. Vigil	48
	Jun 24	St. John the Baptist	50
	Jun 25-27	Ordinary Compline	2-15
	Jun 28	Sts. Peter & Paul Vigil	48
	Jun 29	Sts. Peter & Paul	50
	Jun 30	Most Sacr. Heart Vigil	48
July	July 1	Sacred Heart	50
	July 1-Aug 14	Ordinary Compline	2-15
Aug	Aug 15	Assumption of Mary	50
	Aug 16-Oct 30	Ordinary Compline	2-15
Oct	Oct 31	All Saints Vigil	48
Nov	Nov 1	All Saints	50
	Nov 2-Dec 6	Ordinary Compline	2-15
	Dec 7	Imm Conception Vigil	48
Dec	Dec 8	Immaculate Conception	50
	Dec 9-Dec 31	Ordinary Compline	2-15

2012

	Date	Celebration	Page
Jan	Jan 1 -Mar 18	Ordinary Compline	2-15
	Mar 19	St. Joseph	50
Mar	Mar 20-25	Ordinary Compline	2-15
	Mar 26	Annunciation	50
	Mar 27-Apr 4	Ordinary Compline	2-15
	Apr 5	Holy Thursday	18
	Apr 6	Good Friday	20
Apr	Apr 7	Holy Saturday	22
	Apr 8-15	Easter Octave	26-29
	Apr 16-May 15	Easter Season	32-45
	May 16	Ascension Vigil	52
May	May 17	Ascension	54
	May 18-27	Easter Season	32-45
	May 28-Jun 13	Ordinary Compline	2-15
	June 14	Most Sacr. Heart Vigil	48
	June 15	Sacred Heart	50
June	Jun 16-27	Ordinary Compline	2-15
	Jun 28	Sts. Peter & Paul Vigil	48
	Jun 29	Sts. Peter & Paul	50
	Jun 30-Aug 13	Ordinary Compline	2-15
	Aug 14	Assumption Vigil	48
Aug	Aug 15	Assumption of Mary	50
	Aug 16-Oct 30	Ordinary Compline	2-15
Oct	Oct 31	All Saints Vigil	48
Nov	Nov 1	All Saints	50
	Nov 2-Dec 6	Ordinary Compline	2-15
	Dec 7	Imm Conception Vigil	48
	Dec 8	Immaculate Conception	50
Dec	Dec 9-Dec 23	Ordinary Compline	2-15
	Dec 24	Christmas Vigil	48
	Dec 25	Christmas	50
	Dec 26-Dec 30	Ordinary Compline	2-15
	Dec 31	Sol. of Mary Vigil	48

Liturgical Calendar

2013

	Date	Celebration	Page
Jan	Jan 1	Solemnity of Mary	50
	Jan 2 -Mar 17	Ordinary Compline	2-15
	Mar 18	St. Joseph Vigil	48
	Mar 19	St. Joseph	50
Mar	Mar 20-27	Ordinary Compline	2-15
	Mar 28	Holy Thursday	18
	Mar 29	Good Friday	20
	Mar 30	Holy Saturday	22
	Mar 31-Apr 7	Easter Octave	26-29
Apr	Apr 8	Annunciation	50
	Apr 9-May 7	Easter Season	32-45
	May 8	Ascension Vigil	52
May	May 9	Ascension	54
	May 10-19	Easter Season	32-45
	May 20-Jun 5	Ordinary Compline	2-15
	Jun 6	Most Sacr. Heart Vigil	48
	Jun 7	Sacred Heart	50
June	Jun 8-27	Ordinary Compline	2-15
	Jun 28	Sts. Peter & Paul Vigil	48
	Jun 29	Sts. Peter & Paul	50
	Jun 30-Aug 13	Ordinary Compline	2-15
	Aug 14	Assumption Vigil	48
Aug	Aug 15	Assumption of Mary	50
	Aug 16-Oct 30	Ordinary Compline	2-15
Oct	Oct 31	All Saints Vigil	48
Nov	Nov 1	All Saints	50
	Nov 2-Dec 7	Ordinary Compline	2-15
	Dec 8	Immaculate Conception	50
	Dec 9-Dec 23	Ordinary Compline	2-15
Dec	Dec 24	Christmas Vigil	48
	Dec 25	Christmas	50
	Dec 26-30	Ordinary Compline	2-15
	Dec 31	Sol. of Mary Vigil	48

2014

	Date	Celebration	Page
Jan	Jan 1	Solemnity of Mary	50
	Jan 2-Mar 17	Ordinary Compline	2-15
	Mar 18	St. Joseph Vigil	48
	Mar 19	St. Joseph	50
Mar	Mar 20-23	Ordinary Compline	2-15
	Mar 24	Annunciation Vigil	48
	Mar 25	Annunciation	50
	Mar 26-Apr 16	Ordinary Compline	2-15
	Apr 17	Holy Thursday	18
Apr	Apr 18	Good Friday	20
	Apr 19	Holy Saturday	22
	Apr 20-27	Easter Octave	26-29
	Apr 28-May 27	Easter Season	32-45
May	May 28	Ascension Vigil	52
	May 29	Ascension	54
	May 30-Jun 7	Easter Season	32-45
	Jun 8-22	Ordinary Compline	2-15
	Jun 23	St. John Bapt. Vigil	48
June	Jun 24	St. John the Baptist	50
	Jun 25	Ordinary Compline	2-15
	Jun 26	Most Sacr. Heart Vigil	48
	Jun 27	Sacred Heart	50
	Jun 28-Aug 13	Ordinary Compline	2-15
	Aug 14	Assumption Vigil	48
Aug	Aug 15	Assumption of Mary	50
	Aug 16-Oct 30	Ordinary Compline	2-15
Oct	Oct 31	All Saints Vigil	48
Nov	Nov 1	All Saints	50
	Nov 2-Dec 7	Ordinary Compline	2-15
	Dec 8	Immaculate Conception	50
	Dec 9-Dec 23	Ordinary Compline	2-15
Dec	Dec 24	Christmas Vigil	48
	Dec 25	Christmas	50
	Dec 26-Dec 30	Ordinary Compline	2-15
	Dec 31	Sol. of Mary Vigil	48

Liturgical Calendar

2015

	Date	Celebration	Page
Jan	Jan 1	Solemnity of Mary	50
	Jan 2 -Mar 17	Ordinary Compline	2-15
	Mar 18	St. Joseph Vigil	48
	Mar 19	St. Joseph	50
Mar	Mar 20-23	Ordinary Compline	2-15
	Mar 24	Annunciation Vigil	48
	Mar 25	Annunciation	50
	Mar 26-Apr 1	Ordinary Compline	2-15
	Apr 2	Holy Thursday	18
	Apr 3	Good Friday	20
Apr	Apr 4	Holy Saturday	22
	Apr 5-12	Easter Octave	26-29
	Apr 13-May 12	Easter Season	32-45
	May 13	Ascension Vigil	52
May	May 14	Ascension	54
	May 15-24	Easter Season	32-45
	May 25-Jun 10	Ordinary Compline	2-15
	Jun 11	Most Sacr. Heart Vigil	48
	Jun 12	Most Sacred Heart	50
	Jun 13-22	Ordinary Compline	2-15
June	Jun 23	St. John Bapt. Vigil	48
	Jun 24	St. John the Baptist	50
	Jun 25-28	Ordinary Compline	2-15
	Jun 29	Sts. Peter & Paul	50
	Jun 30-Aug 13	Ordinary Compline	2-15
	Aug 14	Assumption Vigil	48
Aug	Aug 15	Assumption of Mary	50
	Aug 16-Dec 6	Ordinary Compline	2-15
	Dec 7	Imm Conception Vigil	48
	Dec 8	Immaculate Conception	50
	Dec 9-23	Ordinary Compline	2-15
Dec	Dec 24	Christmas Vigil	48
	Dec 25	Christmas	50
	Dec 26-30	Ordinary Compline	2-15
	Dec 31	Sol. of Mary Vigil	48

2016

	Date	Celebration	Page
Jan	Jan 1	Solemnity of Mary	50
	Jan 2 -Mar 17	Ordinary Compline	2-15
	Mar 18	St. Joseph Vigil	48
	Mar 19	St. Joseph	50
Mar	Mar 20-23	Ordinary Compline	2-15
	Mar 24	Holy Thursday	18
	Mar 25	Good Friday	20
	Mar 26	Holy Saturday	22
	Mar 27-Apr 3	Easter Octave	26-29
Apr	Apr 4	Annunciation	54
	Apr 5-May 3	Easter Season	32-45
	May 4	Ascension Vigil	52
May	May 5	Ascension	54
	May 6-15	Easter Season	32-45
	May 16- Jun 1	Ordinary Compline	2-15
	June 2	Most Sacr. Heart Vigil	48
	June 3	Sacred Heart	50
	Jun 4-22	Ordinary Compline	2-15
	Jun 23	St. John Bapt. Vigil	48
June	Jun 24	St. John the Baptist	50
	Jun 25-27	Ordinary Compline	2-15
	Jun 28	Sts. Peter & Paul Vigil	48
	Jun 29	Sts. Peter & Paul	50
	Jun 30-Aug 14	Ordinary Compline	2-15
Aug	Aug 15	Assumption of Mary	50
	Aug 16-Oct 30	Ordinary Compline	2-15
Oct	Oct 31	All Saints Vigil	48
Nov	Nov 1	All Saints	50
	Nov 2-Dec 6	Ordinary Compline	2-15
	Dec 7	Imm. Comception Vigil	48
Dec	Dec 8	Immaculate Conception	50
	Dec 9-Dec 31	Ordinary Compline	2-15

ABOUT THE ST. THOMAS MORE HOUSE OF PRAYER

The Saint Thomas More House of Prayer was founded for the purpose of praying and promoting the Liturgy of the Hours among the laity. The House of Prayer is hidden away in the little village of Van, Pennsylvania. At the House, all of the Hours are prayed throughout the day, rooms are available for overnight retreats and the Blessed Sacrament is present in the chapel—all for the spiritual edification of the faithful. A separate apartment is available for priests who would like to come for retreat and to assist in the mission of the House. For more information call 814-676-1910 or visit our website at www.liturgyofthehours.org.

ABOUT SACROS

As part of its efforts to promote the Liturgy of the Hours, the St. Thomas More House of Prayer has teamed up with Sacros (formerly Patmos), a publishing group led by Anthony Mioni of Shohola, Pennsylvania, to create this unique prayerbook. Other helpful products may be found on the Sacros website at www.sacros.com.